First published 1975
Published by William Collins Sons and Company Limited, Glasgow and London
© 1975 Robert Tyndall Ltd
Printed in Spain
by E. Belgas, S. L. Bilbao - Spain
ISBN 0 00 106136 4

The Story of Flight

Roy Allen

Drawings by Jack Pelling

Collins

Glasgow and London

The publishers wish to express their
grateful thanks to the following for
permission to reproduce photographs
on the pages mentioned:
Associated Press (page 20);
Radio Times Hulton Picture Library (page 23);
Smith's Industries Ltd (page 41);
British Overseas Airways Corporation (page 43).

CONTENTS

Introduction	9
The first attempts to fly	10
The first aircraft—and the men who flew them	14
The first long-distance flights	17
Modern aircraft and how we use them	22
The jet engine	23
Radar	26
The machmeter	27
Pressurization	27
Helicopters	28
Aircraft for special purposes	29
Gliders	30
Warplanes since the Second World War	31
Fighters	31
Bombers and transport planes	36
Civil aircraft	41
Catering	43
Airliners	44
Supersonic passenger flight	51
Rocket-powered craft	53
The space age	55
Diary of important dates	58
Glossary	59
Index	60

INTRODUCTION

Since man's earliest days on planet Earth he has wanted to fly. Although he realised that birds alone were equipped to soar, to travel through the air and to hover, man nevertheless felt that he could rise above his earth-bound limitations and copy the birds. So he pursued his ambition.

His attempts continued for about 2500 years, but it was not until the nineteenth century that man really began to put his beliefs to workable experiments. Quite correctly, he threw out fanciful ideas for ascending machines and what we would now call vertical take-off and landing, and he abandoned flapping wings as something truly belonging to the birds! Man came to see that the best way of lifting himself into the air was by building sails or kites big enough to carry him.

When he had confirmed this momentous discovery by building man-carrying gliders his next step was to apply power to the craft for propulsive purposes. So he built engines and fixed them to his gliders. From then on he moved forward at a fantastic pace. He built bigger, faster aircraft and flew them at increasingly high altitudes. In the space of 80 years man's accumulated knowledge has enabled him to leave the Earth's atmosphere and its gravitational pull: he could leave his natural planet home and fly to the moon.

Man's achievements in the field of flight over the past hundred years make an amazing story—one of the most important episodes in his entire history.

Hawker Siddeley Harrier

Opposite:
1 *First European flight, Santos-Dumont 14 bis, 1906;*
2 *First monocoque aeroplane, the Deperdussin Racer, 1912-13;*
3 *Junkers JU52/3M;*
4 *Sud-Aviation Caravelle II (prototype 1955, production aircraft 1958);*
5 *European A-300B 'Airbus' (Britain-France-West Germany prototype 1972);*
6 *Dornier DO 31 E V/STOL, 1967;*
7 *Saab 37 Viggen (prototype 1967);*
8 *BAC-Sud-Aviation Concorde, 1974;*
9 *BAC-Breguet Jaguar prototype 1968.*

THE FIRST ATTEMPTS TO FLY

As the most intelligent creature on Earth, there are not many feats man has not attempted in the course of his evolution. After a gradual process of trial and error, he had many times done 'the impossible'. So it was with flying. Man is now reckoned to have been on Earth for about two and a half million years, and it is only in the last 70 to 80 years that he has mastered flight—but he was certainly thinking about it some 4000 years ago. About 2200 BC the Chinese emperor Shun leaped from the top of a tower and descended safely with the aid of two large reed hats. You could say that this story only proves that the parachute was on the way as an invention, but flying was definitely in the emperor's mind!

Many other stories have been handed down through the ages. One of these in Greek mythology concerns Daedalus and Icarus, who, to escape from prison, made themselves wings of feathers and wax. They were successful in their flight, but elation led them to disaster. Icarus flew too near the sun—the heat melted the wax on his wings, he fell into the sea and was drowned.

Another story tells of Bladud, the flying king of Britain, who in 852 BC fell and broke his neck while making an attempt to fly like emperor Shun. Not until the end of the fifteenth century did true science replace mythology and so-called magic. The great Leonardo da Vinci used the simple scientific knowledge of the time to make drawings and calculations for a man-carrying aircraft, which was to fly under the power of flapping wings. He also invented a helicopter of a sort, a spring-operated flying machine and a parachute. Da Vinci wrote about his work in Florence in 1505, but his writings were not published until 1797—by which time man had made the first aerial journey. But this was in a balloon, a device which da Vinci had not considered.

Two flying machines designed by Leonardo da Vinci. Above: the Ornithopter; below: the Helicopter

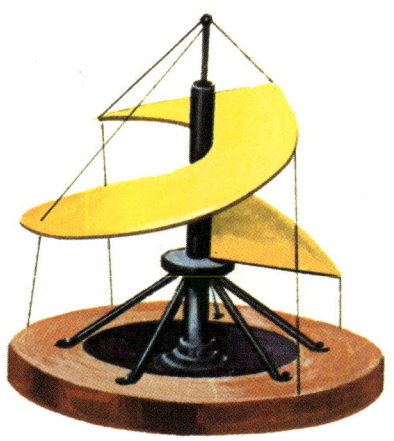

Between da Vinci's skilful drawings and the first practical work on flying machines, over 260 years elapsed. Men involved in flight experiments still based their work on their observations of birds. Then, in 1782, two brothers in France, Joseph and Etienne Montgolfier, took up an interest in flying. They had never heard of Leonardo da Vinci, but they *had* heard about gas. At that time, people were experimenting with hydrogen gas, which the English chemist Henry Cavendish had discovered was lighter than the air we breathe.

Hydrogen gas balloons, and also hot air balloons, were being tested. Tiberius Cavallo, a Fellow of the Royal Society in London, tried out a hydrogen balloon in 1782 with only partial success. It was left to the Montgolfier brothers to produce the first balloon actually to rise from the ground, and this they demonstrated in June 1783. Made of linen and lined with paper, the balloon rose when a bonfire of straw and wool was lit below it, thus trapping hot air in the envelope. The brothers believed that this fuel, together with hot air, produced a special gas which they called Montgolfier's gas, but it was, of course, nothing more than hot air. Nevertheless, this was sufficient to lift the balloon and by September 1783 the brothers were able to send up in a wicker basket a sheep, a cock and a duck. On 15 October 1783 they were responsible for the first ascent ever by a human being.

Using a Montgolfier balloon, a doctor named J.F. Pilâtre de Rozier made a number of ascents and kept himself up for minutes at a time by stoking the brazier. However, his balloon was tethered to the ground by ropes. Then, on 21 November 1783 the doctor and a cavalry officer, the Marquis d'Arlandes, made the first free flight by men recorded in history. They started from the Bois de Boulogne in Paris and flew across the city

The top balloon was designed by Henry Coxwell in 1848. The one above is a steam-driven balloon designed in 1852 by Henry Gifford.

where they landed on the other side of the River Seine.

This achievement inspired other balloonists. The hot air balloons of the Montgolfiers were followed by the lighter hydrogen balloons of J.A.C. Charles and others. Men *and* women made balloon

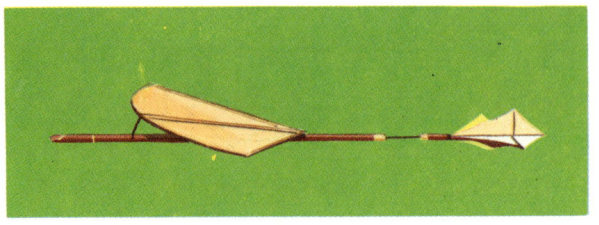
George Cayley's model kite

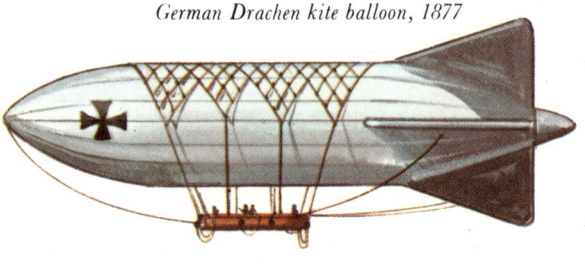
German Drachen kite balloon, 1877

George Cayley's glider

Otto Lilienthal glider, 1891–2

flights. Balloons became bigger, and were used for races, sporting events and then war. In January 1785 the English Channel was crossed for the first time by air, with a balloon manned by Dr J. Jeffries and Monsieur J.P. Blanchard. In 1848 the first air raid was made using small hot air balloons, each carrying a thirteen-kilogramme (30-pound) bomb. These were drifted over Venice by the Austrian army. In 1890 a British army balloon unit was formed.

Meanwhile, the study of man-carrying flight had taken another direction. An Englishman, Sir George Cayley, was working along lines similar to da Vinci's. He built models for flying research work, designed a vertical take-off aircraft, and in 1853 constructed a full-sized glider which was said to be capable of carrying a boy. Sir George Cayley is acknowledged as the father of aeronautics, and his influence on the aviation pioneers was tremendous. Much of what the Wright brothers and others were to practise years later, Sir George Cayley had written about in the mid 1850s.

Yet, not until the end of the nineteenth century did the first man-carrying gliders appear. In 1891, a German, Otto Lilienthal, built with his brother Gustav a monoplane glider which had a wing area of about 11 square metres (110 square feet). Lilienthal enjoyed some success with this glider, but better things were in store in 1895, with the introduction of biplanes. Lilienthal made numerous glides at Berlin and Stollen, and sometimes he flew at more than 230 metres (750 feet). But his method of hanging from beneath the wings and controlling the glider by moving his body ended in a fatal accident when his glider crashed in 1896.

Other pioneers of the time included an Englishman, Percy Pilcher; a Frenchman who had gone

Zeppelin of 1900 and the Wright brothers' biplane, The Flyer

to the United States as a boy, Octave Chanute; and an Australian, Lawrence Hargrave, who was following his own distinct line of enquiry with man-lifting kites. Hargrave was one of the most important aeronautical designers, as his box kites formed the basis for the first successful aircraft. These were made by the Wright brothers, in Dayton, Ohio, USA.

At the turn of the century the two brothers—who made and repaired bicycles for a living—started experiments with aircraft. They first made a glider of five metres (seventeen feet) wing span which they flew as a kite. Then they moved on to larger gliders, and by 1902 were gliding over long distances of over 182 metres (600 feet) with one of them on board. The next step was to fit an engine to a glider for propulsion, and this they did in 1903. The Wright brothers had enormous difficulty finding an engine that was light enough and yet sufficiently powerful to install in their aircraft. They finally decided to build their own twelve-horse-power engine, a very remarkable achievement for the time.

In 1903, the brothers had moved to Kitty Hawk, North Carolina, because of the favourable winds for flying, and by December of that year their machine was ready. After a twelve-metre (40-feet) take-off run, and travelling at about 12 kmph (8 mph), the Wright brothers' aircraft, called the *Flyer*, took off and flew, on 17 December 1903. It covered 36 metres (120 feet), and it was the first time in the history of man that a man-carrying aircraft had taken off under its own power, flown under control and landed at the same height at which it took off. This was an achievement which astonished the world.

THE FIRST AIRCRAFT—AND THE MEN WHO FLEW THEM

The success of the Wrights in America left the rest of the world rather breathless. In those days, news about even major events travelled slowly, and it took some time for the magnitude of the event to penetrate; in many quarters it was just not believed.

This was partly the case with Europe, for so many aeronautical experiments had been going on in Europe for so long, that the aspiring airmen on the continent felt a little cheated by the news from America. In France they just would not believe it! A Frenchman, Clément Ader, had in 1890 made what amounted to a leap off the ground in a powered aeroplane of his own design, called the *Eole*. He covered 50 metres (165 feet) before flopping back on the ground, and in 1897 tried again without success. But this first, tentative flight was a mere 13 years before the Wright brothers made history. No wonder the French would not believe these upstart Americans!

Elsewhere in Europe there had been much flying activity. In 1901 a Brazilian, Alberto Santos-Dumont had flown around the Eiffel Tower in an airship driven by a twelve hp automobile engine. In November 1906 he was to graduate to powered flight in an aeroplane. Aviators all over Europe were on the brink of making flights with their own aircraft—but most of these machines owed their design features to the Wright brothers' biplanes.

The reason for the suspicious attitudes towards the Wrights' success resulted from the great

Demoiselle monoplane, 1907

Voisin biplane, 1909

Blériot's XI monoplane crossing the English Channel in 1909

secrecy with which the two Americans shrouded their work. When they first made experimental glides, people would not stop pestering them, yet when they succeeded in putting an engine in their biplane glider and making regular, controlled flights their announcement in a newspaper aroused no interest. After this they became secretive. But when they arrived in Europe in 1908 to demonstrate their *Flyer* on the fields of France, the whole of Europe was astounded. There was no doubt now who could really fly—and who flew first!

The tremendous upsurge in flying all over Europe led to many claims of various first flights. A Dane, J.C.H. Ellehammer, flew on the island of Lindholm in September 1906. In November of that year Alberto Santos-Dumont made a definitive flight with his biplane in the Bois de Boulogne, Paris. This meant the flight was observed officially. The Voisin brothers in France were now building biplanes, and in England experimenters such as A.V. Roe were progressing. The Voisin aeroplanes were flying by 1907, and in June 1908 A.V. Roe became the first Englishman to fly in England, with a biplane he had designed and built himself. Then in 1909 Louis Blériot arrived on the scene.

Blériot, a manufacturer of motor car headlamps, had turned to flying from interest and also for the financial rewards it offered. One such reward was the £1000 offered by the British *Daily Mail* newspaper to the first man who could fly across the English Channel. Blériot, who had concentrated on the design of monoplanes rather than the standard biplanes, decided to enter the competition. After a brief test flight in Calais, he took off in the early morning of Sunday 25 July 1909 and flew off across the Channel, landing in England, near Dover Castle, 37 minutes later. He was met by a Customs officer who was more concerned about checking his possessions than in congratulating him on his brilliant achievement! Blériot's monoplane had a wing span of eight and a half metres (28 feet) and an engine of 25 hp. His success brought him world-wide fame, and orders for about a hundred of his planes.

1909 was a red-letter year in aviation history. Many aircraft construction companies were founded, the world's first air meeting took place at Reims, France, and the very first Paris Aero Show was held. A number of historic flights were also made.

Now flying had caught the interest of the public in a big way. The balloon was still popular, and was to return to the scene as an air transport vehicle ten years later, but the aeroplane was the wonder of the age. Races and competitions were

Paulhan's victorious arrival in Manchester in 1910

15

organized and flying meetings were held all over the world, in Barcelona, Berlin, St Petersburg (Leningrad), Heliopolis in Egypt and in the United States, where the Wright brothers and another designer and builder, Glen Curtiss, competed with each other.

In 1910 the London *Daily Mail* organized another competition—£10,000 to be awarded to the first man to fly from London to Manchester in the north of England—a distance of 296 kilometres (184 miles). The flight had to be completed within 24 hours. A Briton, Claude Grahame-White, put up a spirited performance, and in the course of his attempt made the first night flight in history; but he was forced out of the race by engine trouble. A Frenchman, Louis Paulhan, was the winner at an average speed of 71 kilometres (44 miles) per hour.

In 1910 another prize, for £4000, was won by T. Sopwith (now Sir Thomas Sopwith) with a flight of 285 kilometres (177 miles) from England to Belgium. In the following year another £10,000 was won from the *Daily Mail* by the successful completion of a 1609 kilometre (1000 mile) round-Britain flight by a lieutenant in the French Navy, J. de Conneau. In 1911 Pierre Prier made the first non-stop flight from London to Paris in four hours 55 minutes. Today the same flight takes 35 minutes! In the same year the first aerial post in Britain was carried from Hendon to Windsor by Gustav Hamel. More than 100,000 letters were carried on this service before it was stopped owing to bad weather and consequent delays to the aircraft.

1911 also witnessed one of the most remarkable long-distance flights in the history of aviation. William Randolph Hearst in America offered $50,000 to the pilot who could complete the first coast-to-coast flight across the United States. Galbraith Rodgers started from New York with a Wright biplane to try to complete the journey in the specified 30 days. He took seven weeks in all, and his journey was a chapter of disasters. He was blown off course, chased by an eagle, and nearly crashed into a mountain. His aeroplane was picked at by souvenir hunters, and he had difficulty in taking off among crowds. At one stage he had to hold the engine together by hand, and his aircraft was repaired so frequently that by the time he arrived in California the only original remaining parts were the rudder and a drip pan!

De Havilland B.E.2 1912–13

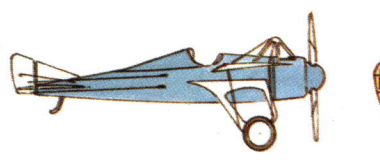

Monocoque Deperdussin, 1912–13

Sikorsky's VS–300, 1942

THE FIRST LONG-DISTANCE FLIGHTS

The German Zeppelin was used in the First World War for night raids over Britain

As Wilbur and Orville Wright said, the age of the flying machine had come at last. Designers and pilots could hardly keep pace with all the many changes and new ideas: every day, longer, faster and higher-flying aircraft appeared. The whole world was caught up in this new age of the aeroplane, for it must not be forgotten that the aeroplane was one of the most advanced craft ever invented. Unlike the ship, the motor car and the railway train, it was a free-ranging vehicle. It could operate in three dimensions, over land, across the seas and in any direction in the air. In another half-century the flying machine would take man through the atmosphere into outer space. But that was still a long way off.

As new designs took to the air in increasing numbers the world over, a shadow was cast across the flying scene by the commencement of the First World War in Europe, in August 1914. Using aeroplanes for war purposes was an idea which few people took seriously, although some thought they could possibly be useful as observation craft, or message-carriers, in the same way that balloons were used to carry messages out of Paris in the Franco-Prussian war of 1870.

However, Orville and Wilbur Wright *did* recognize the military value of their aeroplanes, and felt that this was a sure way to obtain funds for developing their machines. In 1903, they had already offered their invention to the US War

Handley Page 0/400, London-Paris 1919

Vickers Vimy, Alcock and Brown 1919

Office, but were turned down. Not until 1909 were they awarded a government contract—although the US government had little conception of the value of the project.

Designers continued to work to make the aeroplane an efficient military machine. Flying had been born in fun and as a sport, and now it was being used for war. European governments were spending vast sums of money turning the aeroplane into a means of killing people and winning wars—as a peaceful machine it had held no interest for them.

Aircraft design improved by leaps and bounds. Planes were fitted with two engines instead of just one, and were built to carry two men and then three. Blériot's machine, which had crossed the Channel, had been capable of a speed of about 97 kilometres (60 miles) per hour, but by the time the Great War ended, fighters existed which could reach 225 kilometres (140 miles) per hour, and some of them gained heights of over 6100 metres (20,000 feet).

Four-engined bombers were built which could carry up to four tons, and both British and German big bombers, with wing spans of 24 metres (80 feet) to 30 metres (100 feet), made long-range flights with their bomb loads, covering 480-570 kilometres (300-350 miles) at a time.

It so happened that a use was found for these big wartime aeroplanes when peace came again. A few men who loved flying and had an eye to the future recognized the possibilities of air passenger services and cargo and mail transport by air— depending, of course, on whether people were prepared to pay for such services. In England, Holland, France and the USA, groups of men got together to form air companies or airlines. No one had ever made passenger-carrying aircraft before, so they modified wartime bombers and transporters by fitting them with passenger seats.

In 1919 services were started between London and Paris; in 1920 between London and Amsterdam and later to Berlin, Prague and Copenhagen. In America, airline services began with regular flights between New York and Boston, Cleveland, Detroit, San Francisco, Los Angeles, Chicago and Miami. So the aeroplane, whose development had been boosted by the war, was now flying people for pleasure and commercial profit in a way which would have seemed impossible just twenty years earlier. Governments everywhere were taking an interest in and backing the new airlines and soon a proper international airmail service was instituted.

Before the Great War ended, aircraft were made larger in order to carry more and fly farther. It was in the interest of a number of men to fly over particularly long distances, and some of these big aircraft were quite suitable for such long-range flying if they carried fuel instead of bombs or stores. Among these flyers were the British Brigadier-General Borton and Major Maclaren, who embarked on a flight to Cairo from England in 1918. They reached their destination in eleven days, and a Captain Ross Smith then flew the same aeroplane from Cairo to Delhi, India, in thirteen days.

Major Maclaren, accompanied this time by a Lieutenant Halley, next embarked on a flight from England to India; using a four-engined Handley Page bomber, they flew to Karachi via Cairo in 1919. This same year an American flying-boat, a Curtiss NC-4, was flown across the Atlantic, from west to east, by a Lieutenant-Commander Read and his crew. They flew in stages, from Newfoundland to Portugal by way of the Azores, and their aircraft was the only one to complete the flight of three which had set out.

In June 1919 one of the finest ever long-distance flights was made. John Alcock and Arthur Whitten Brown set out from St John's, Newfoundland in a Vickers Vimy bomber to fly non-stop to Britain. The aircraft was powered by two Rolls-Royce Eagle engines and extra fuel tanks had been fitted. The men took off from Newfoundland in bright sunshine but soon ran into dense fog. Brown was navigating. He set a course which they followed for hours until, catching a glimpse of the stars through the clouds he realised that now, at night, they were on a true course over the Atlantic.

In spite of the fact that it was June, snow and sleet fell and ice formed on the aircraft's wings. The weight of this, which destroyed the lift of the wings, caused the aircraft to spin down to the sea, and it was only 30 metres (100 feet) above the Atlantic when Alcock regained control. Though exhausted, the two men carried on, and saw land on the morning of 15 June. Thinking this was England, they landed, but were disappointed to find themselves in Clifden, County Galway, Ireland. Their flight across the Atlantic

Alan Cobham's D.H.50, 1926

The ill-fated Hindenburg

—the first ever made non-stop in an aeroplane—had taken fifteen hours 57 minutes, at an average speed of 192 kilometres (119 miles) per hour. A statue to their memory now stands at Heathrow Airport, London.

Three weeks after Alcock and Brown's flight in the Vimy, the British rigid airship R-34 made a remarkable first east-west crossing of the Atlantic. It flew from Scotland to New York in four and a half days, and three days later made the return trip. The airship was an in-between type of aircraft, one which had a mixed career before it was finally abandoned. Following the Great War, many commercial airships were built.

A German Count, Ferdinand Zeppelin, believed that the large rigid airship was a safe and modern vehicle for long-range passenger flights, and he set about proving this to the world by building a number of very large airships, which became known as Zeppelins.

Zeppelins were very successfully used for passenger services throughout the 1920s and 1930s. The most famous of them, the *Graf Zeppelin*, was 235 metres (772 feet) long and 30 metres (100 feet) in diameter. She carried a 40-strong crew and twenty passengers, and flew at 128 kilometres (80 miles) per hour. During her career, the *Graf Zeppelin* made 590 flights—144 of which were ocean crossings—and carried 13,000 passengers over a million miles. One flight, covering 6410 kilometres (3960 miles), was the longest ever made by an airship.

Zeppelins and airships generally had a big weakness in that their enormous gas-filled bodies were vulnerable to fire. The *Graf Zeppelin* showed that airships could be safely used, but after four accidents involving American, British and German airships, they were abandoned as too dangerous. Hydrogen gas was gradually being replaced by the non-inflammable gas helium, but this did not prevent the aeroplane from being preferred.

In 1919 another long-distance flight of note was made. The Australian government offered a £10,000 prize to the first Australians to fly from England to Australia in a British aircraft, in under 30 days. Two brothers named Ross and Keith Smith decided to compete in a converted Vimy bomber. They flew the 17,700 kilometres (11,000 miles) from London to Darwin in just under 28 days, and won the prize. Like Alcock and Brown they were knighted.

The first flight from London to South Africa was made in 1920, and then in 1924 four US Army Douglas biplanes set off from Seattle, in Washington State, to fly around the world by way of Alaska, India, Turkey, Austria, Britain, Iceland, Greenland and Labrador. Two of them completed the round trip, flying a total of 44,250 kilometres (27,500 miles).

In 1925 Sir Alan Cobham flew from London to Cape Town, South Africa, in a de Havilland 50 aeroplane with a single Armstrong Siddeley Jaguar engine. He took six weeks on the outgoing journey but returned in the following year in a mere fifteen days. In 1926 he flew from London to Australia and back, covering 45,000 kilometres (28,000 miles). On his return, he alighted on the river Thames, right in front of the Houses of Parliament.

In May 1927 another remarkable flight was made by an American, Charles Lindbergh, who took off from New York in a little Ryan monoplane to fly solo across the Atlantic. His aeroplane, called the *Spirit of St Louis,* carried so much fuel that a special tank had been built in the nose of the aeroplane, effectively blocking the pilot's forward vision. The only way Lindbergh could see forward was by way of a special periscope arrangement. He landed at Le Bourget Airfield, Paris, $33\frac{1}{2}$ hours after taking off from New York and covering 5630 kilometres (3600 miles).

Another solo pilot, H.J. Hinkler, flew in 1928 from England to Australia in fifteen days; in the same year Charles Ulm and Sir Charles Kingsford Smith flew across the Pacific from California to Australia, by way of Hawaii and Fiji, in a three-engined Fokker monoplane, called the *Southern Cross.* A lady pilot, Amy Johnson, made a nineteen day solo flight from England to Australia in a DH Moth. Amelia Earhart was the first woman to cross the Atlantic by air when she flew in 1932 from Newfoundland to Ireland in a Lockheed Vega monoplane.

The North Pole and later the South Pole were flown over, adding to the excitement of this most exciting time, when new records were being made and bettered every day.

Charles Kingsford Smith's Fokker monoplane, 1928

MODERN AIRCRAFT AND HOW WE USE THEM

Spitfire

Mitsubishi

Messerschmitt

Piaggio

Junkers JU.88

B17 Flying Fortress

Avro Lancaster

Heinkel HE178, the first turbo-powered aeroplane to fly (27 August 1939)

Gloster Whittle E28/39, Britain's first jet aeroplane

The days of peace and experiments in long-distance flying vanished abruptly with the start of the Second World War in 1939. Commercial airline services came to a halt in most parts of the world, with the exception of the USA.

Aircraft production was once more geared to military work. Fighters, bombers and war transports alone were produced, which meant that airliner design was neglected. But the urgent need for better, more efficient vehicles also meant that aeroplane design in general made a big leap forward, in the same way as it had in 1914-18. Many complicated inventions appeared, like the jet engine, radar, rocket propulsion for aircraft, the instrument landing system, an aerodrome fog dispersal system called FIDO, and a method of escape for pilots called the ejection seat. There were also many advances in radio communications, specifically for flying, and also in materials.

The Jet Engine

When the Wright brothers made an engine for their first powered aeroplane, they created what was virtually a motor car engine. The internal combustion engine was still quite new then—the first petrol engine to drive a motor car had appeared in 1885. Until then there had been coal engines, gas engines and experiments with steam engines for aeroplanes, although none was successful. The first petrol engine was fitted into an aeroplane in 1902, and this event was followed by a 35 year period of development, during which engines became bigger and more sophisticated.

But a handful of inventors in different countries believed that other kinds of engine could power aeroplanes and among these were the rocket and the gas turbine engine. The rocket was soon found to be unsuitable: for one thing, it was unreliable, as the type of fuel used for combustion made the burning difficult to control. But the gas turbine engine appeared very promising for a number of reasons. It enabled aircraft to fly very fast, its fuel was cheap and its construction was relatively simple.

In the late 1930s, several men were experimenting with turbine-propelled engines. A German named Hans von Ohain put his turbo engine in an aircraft in 1939 and an Italian aeroplane, a Caproni-Campini, flew with an internal engine called a ducted fan. An Englishman, Frank Whittle successfully tested his own jet engine in 1937, and when an improved version was fitted to the Gloster E 28/39, it became the first really successful jet. It flew in May 1941.

Group Captain Frank Whittle

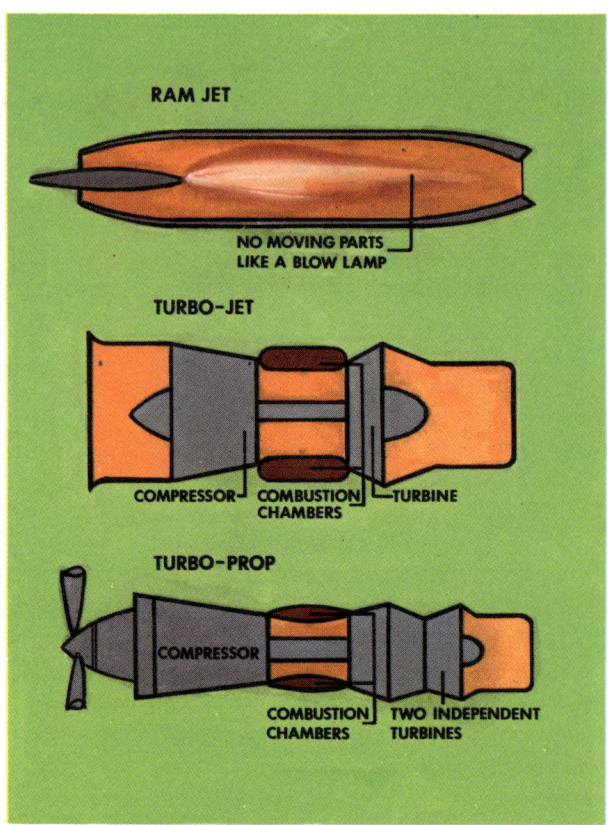

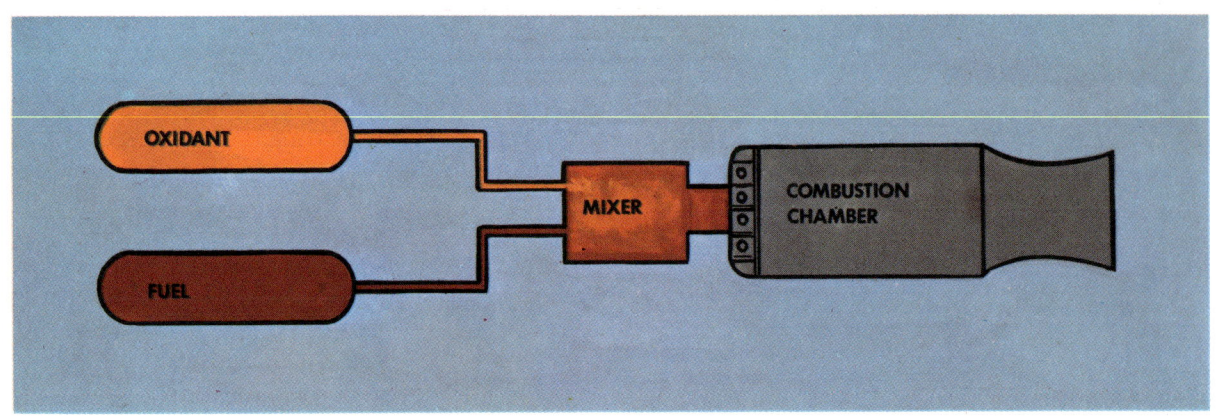

Rocket engine

The gas turbine engine was quickly called the jet engine because of the way the 'pure' jet works. It takes in air at the front, which is quickly mixed with fuel and ignited. In the combustion chamber the lighted fuel changes into hot gases, which expand and force themselves out at the back of the engine in a hot jet. The force of the gases rushing out, as the result of this internal explosion, has the effect of pushing the engine—and the aircraft it is attached to—in the opposite direction, that is forward. As far as the designers of the early days were concerned, this meant they could control the forward movement of the aeroplane by varying the amount of fuel that was burned, and also by the way in which the exhaust gases were thrust out the back.

Jet engines were soon made which were capable of such tremendous forward thrust that they could propel very heavy loads quite fast. It was not many years before the gas turbine—or jet—fighter was joined by the jet airliner and bomber. The military value of the jet engine can be readily understood. It made fighters and bombers a good deal faster than those equipped with propeller engines. After the war, the jet airliner became popular because it enabled people to fly from place to place in a few hours.

There are three main types of jet engine. The 'pure' jet, so called because it works in the way described above, consists of an engine case containing the starter motor, turbines, combustion chambers and the fuel burners. Frank Whittle's engine developed only a few hundred pounds of thrust, but jet engines today reach 50,000 pounds of thrust.

The turbo-prop engine is really a gas turbine engine which drives a propeller. Instead of the main thrust being generated by a hot air jet at the rear, the combustion is translated into driving a shaft with a propeller at the front There is also some slight jet thrust, but the main energy comes from the propeller being turned by the engine. There is more control with a propeller at slow speeds, and this results in more economical flight than pure, high-speed jet flight.

Then there is the ram jet engine. Used for very high-speed flight, it has really found little application so far except on missiles. It is essentially a hollow tube containing burners. Fuel is burnt in this tube when air is pushed through it at very high speed, and the result is a very high-speed flying stovepipe, as it has been called. The ram jet is incapable of flying at slow speeds simply because it cannot take in sufficient air to drive the unit forward. It therefore has to have another engine—or a high-speed vehicle—to take it into the air and reach its necessary operating speed. The combination of a turbo-jet and ram jet can make an incredibly fast vehicle.

A fourth type of jet engine in extensive use today is the by-pass or fan jet. This is really a development of the jet engine. It has an inner sleeve through which air passes, avoiding the combustion process. It by-passes the main flow, in fact. This engine is more economical than the pure jet. The big fan engines of today are both highly efficient and quiet for the power they generate.

Finally, the rocket engine of today must be mentioned. This is not a jet engine at all, of course. It operates completely independently of the outside air for it carries its own supply of oxygen. Rocket fuel, which nowadays is greatly improved, may be in either liquid or solid form. Rockets have been the means of taking space-ships to the moon, for the simple reason that they can operate in outer space, outside the Earth's atmosphere, which encloses the air we breathe.

Radar

Radar, a word made from the phrase: radio direction finding and range, was invented by a Scotsman, Sir Robert Watson-Watt, and first planned as an aid to identifying aircraft in 1935. Radio signals are used to form images, or an electronic picture, on a screen. The viewer can interpret these images, and in the case of aviation, aircraft or clouds can be seen from a distance of many miles. With the help of radar, an aircraft can be guided from the ground by an air traffic controller even though it may be dark or cloudy, or the aircraft is miles away. Commercial air traffic follows certain routes between cities, and these air lanes are under radar control.

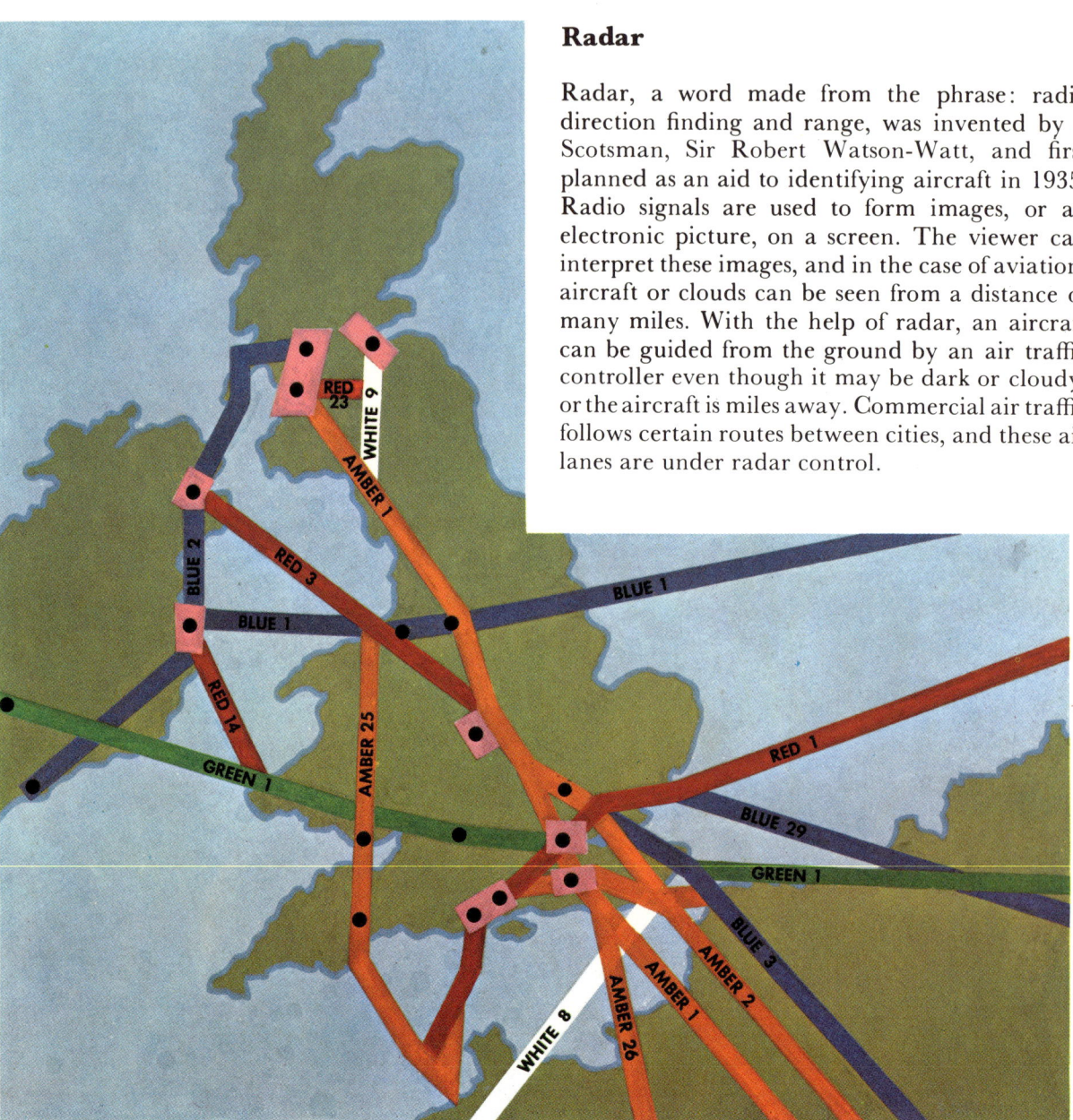

The Machmeter

In all high-speed aircraft today there is a familiar instrument called the Machmeter. Named after an Austrian, Ernst Mach, this instrument expresses the aeroplane's speed as a percentage of the speed of sound. The speed of sound is 1195 kilometres (743 miles) per hour at sea level and at 10,972 metres (36,000 feet) it is 1046 kilometres (650 miles) per hour, above which it is constant. It falls off with altitude because it is related to temperature. An aeroplane flying at 1046 kilometres per hour at 12,000 metres will therefore be flying at Mach 1, or at the same speed at which sound travels at that height. On the Machmeter this will register with the needle against the figure 1. But if the pilot accelerates his aircraft to fly faster than sound, that is, at supersonic speed, and increases his speed to 1150 kilometres (715 miles) per hour, he will be flying at Mach 1·1, or the speed of sound plus ten per cent.

This means he has left sound behind. It catches up in the form of a bang, known as the sonic boom, which is heard on the ground. The reason for this boom is that the aircraft has broken through an invisible shock barrier in the sky. Aircraft are designed to fly at certain speeds around this barrier—or Mach 1—and their structures are called Mach limited. It is therefore important that they do not fly faster than their structures can withstand, hence the importance of the Machmeter.

Above right: diagram of an aircraft passing through the sound barrier

Opposite: radar air lanes

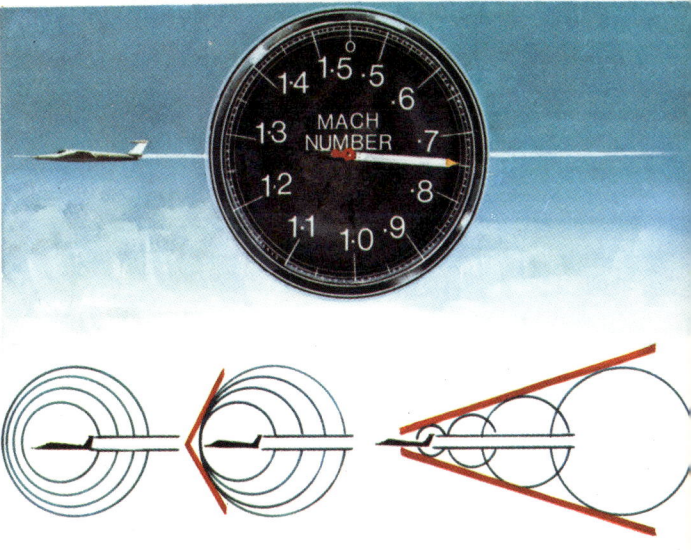

Pressurization

Above 3050 metres (10,000 feet) the density of air is much lower than at sea level. If you fly at this height and above, you will need an artificial supply of oxygen to make up what the air lacks.

Aircraft designers have solved this problem in an ingenious way, by maintaining the same density of air inside airliners when flying high as when flying below 3050 metres. Aircraft are inflated very gently, like a balloon, so that they are pressurized. Most airliners flying today have this artificial atmosphere so that they can fly high and still permit passengers to breathe normally. Pressurization of an airliner's cabin is so cleverly controlled that no one notices the difference in atmospheric pressure.

Aircraft choose to fly at great heights to avoid cloud masses lower down, and because air-breathing engines, like the jet, burn less fuel when the air is thinner. Economy is important; a jet engine consumes hundreds of gallons of fuel an hour.

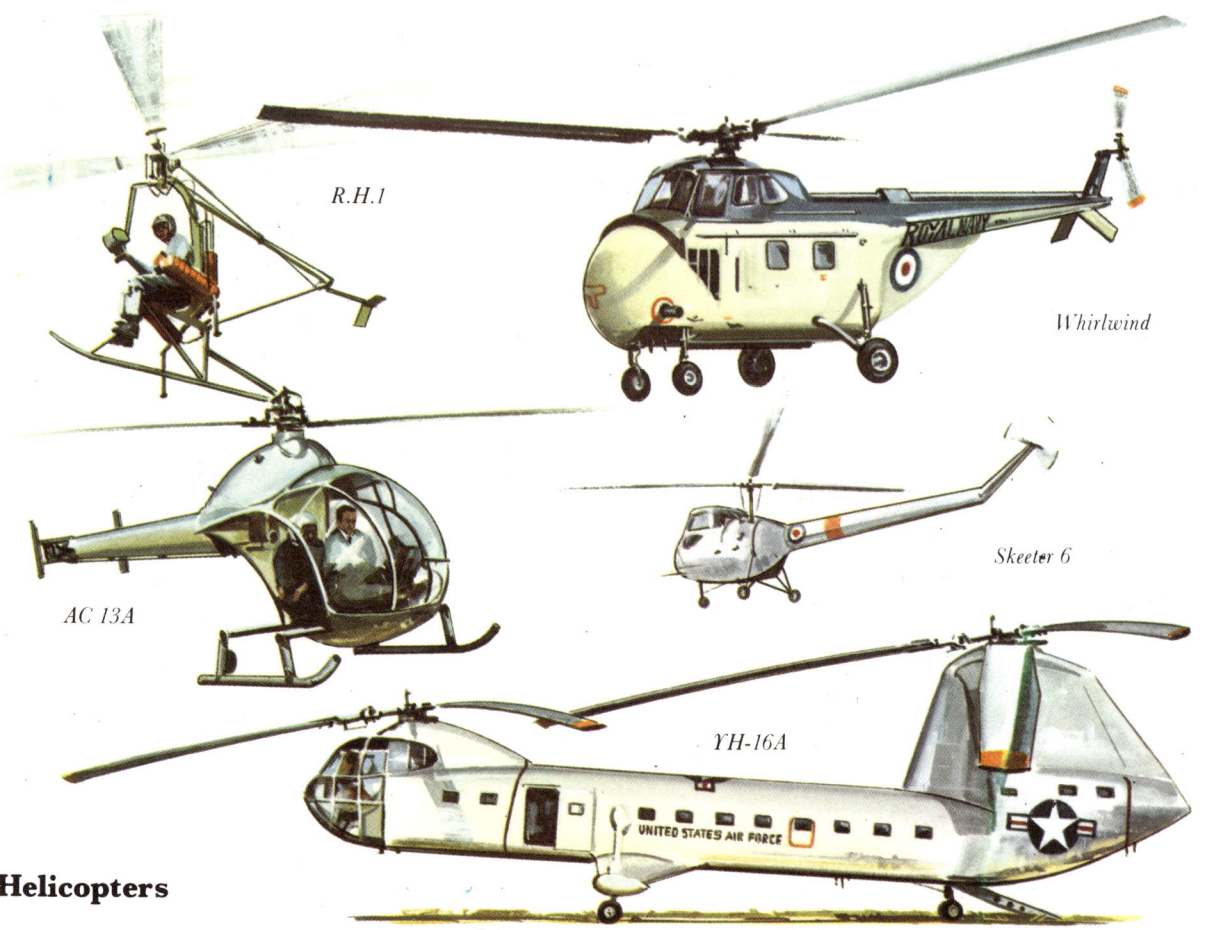

R.H.1
Whirlwind
AC 13A
Skeeter 6
YH-16A

Helicopters

The helicopter is one of the cleverest inventions of man's conquest of the air, for it can do so many things that the fixed-wing aircraft cannot. It imitates birds in the way that man had desired for so many centuries—by standing still in mid-air, or by hovering.

The fixed-wing aeroplane has wings on its fuselage from which it gains lift, climbs and flies along. The engines which drive aircraft are substantially aided in normal flight by the lift from the aeroplane's wings. In the case of the helicopter, however, its engine or engines drive rotors with blades on them. When these blades are turned at certain angles they lift the helicopter and its load, and by combining the angles of the blades against the air with their speed of rotation, it becomes possible for the helicopter to hover, and then fly off in any direction.

The helicopter's development goes right back to Leonardo da Vinci, but the first one to lift off the ground was in 1909. Since then, many thousands of helicopters of different kinds have been built, but particularly since 1940. In that year, a Russian named Igor Sikorsky, living in America, built the first truly successful helicopter, on which all subsequent models are based.

Helicopters have multi-purpose activities in war and in peace. In rescue work, they lift wounded soldiers and sick civilians, and pull people out of the sea. They help to build bridges, erect radio towers and take equipment and men into small fields or even the middle of cities. While costly to operate compared with the fixed-wing aircraft, the helicopter is an aircraft for special duties, and one which is in wide use today. In the future, it is likely to be succeeded by the jet-engined VTOL aircraft, that is, Vertical Take-Off and Landing. This aircraft has a number of advantages over the helicopter, the most important of which is that it hovers by the use of its jet engines, and can function without fragile helicopter rotor blades.

Aircraft for special purposes

Early aeroplanes started by carrying just one or two people, then gradually developed to accommodate mail, stores and more passengers. Later, weapons of war, such as bombs, guns and rockets were transported. Peace-time purposes gave the aeroplane its chance to show just what a unique vehicle it was, however. People soon realised that the flying machine could take goods and passengers to otherwise inaccessible places, and this was particularly true in the case of the helicopter.

But a number of aircraft have been specifically designed for individual tasks. They include the crop-spraying aircraft, used for agricultural purposes; the car-ferry aircraft, designed to carry people and their motor cars across stretches of water; the air ambulance aeroplane, which serves to carry injured or sick people to hospital. The latter usually has a wide cabin into which stretchers can easily be lifted. Helicopters are frequently employed in mountain rescue work, or similar situations where other aircraft are helpless.

In Australia, the air ambulance service reached a peak of perfection with an organization called the Flying Doctor Service. Founded in the 1920s to help doctors reach patients in isolated towns or villages, the service became so important that it is now a full-sized organization rather like an airline, and is equipped with its own special aircraft.

Aircraft are used for many special purposes, ranging from aerial fire fighting, police patrol work and road traffic control. In some countries, helicopters have been used to chase bank robbers!

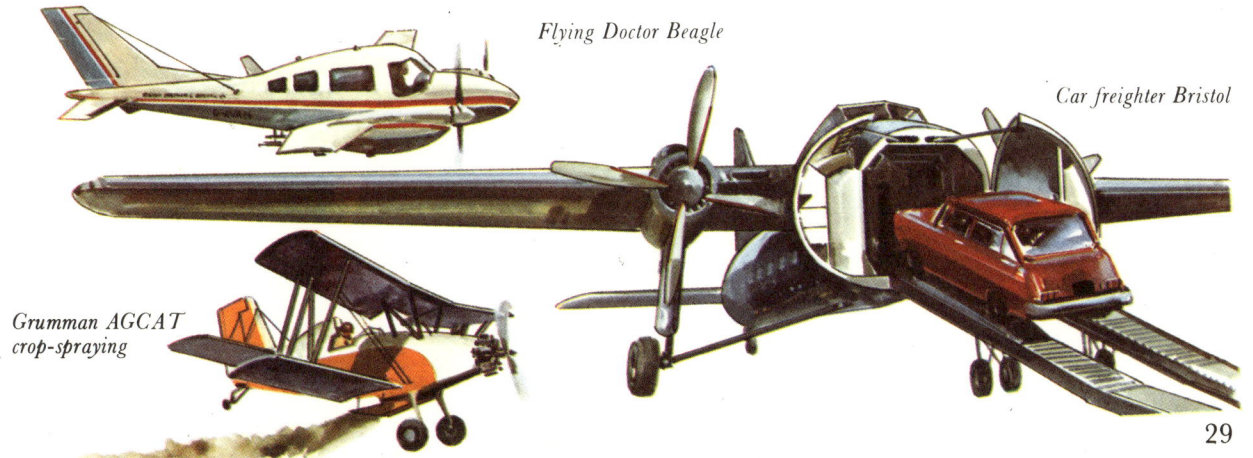

Flying Doctor Beagle

Car freighter Bristol

Grumman AGCAT crop-spraying

GLIDERS

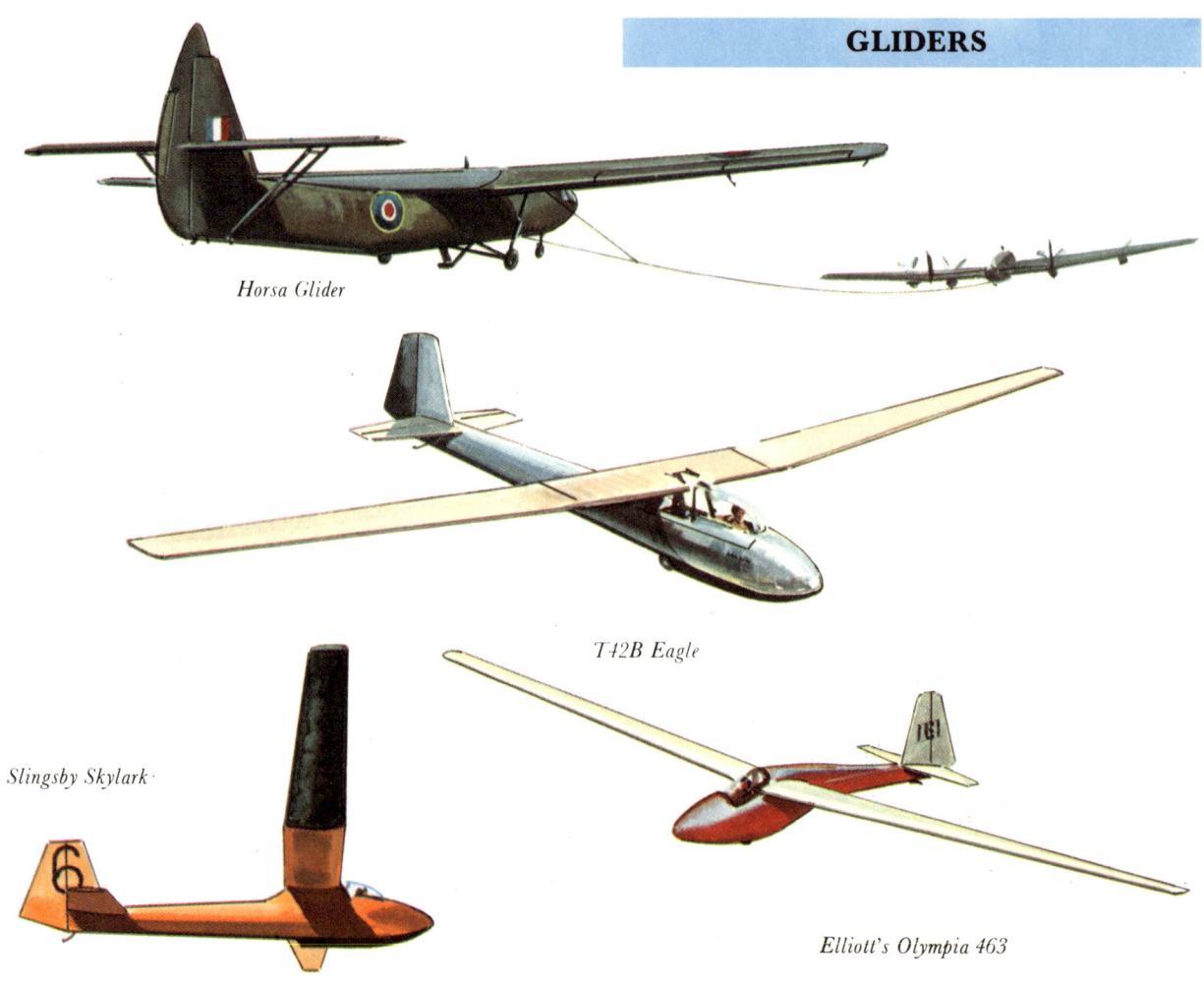

Horsa Glider

T42B Eagle

Slingsby Skylark

Elliott's Olympia 463

Today the glider is used almost only for sport and pleasure, but we must remember that it was the *first* successful aeroplane. The Wright brothers' *Flyer* was really a glider with an engine in it, and so were many of the pioneer aircraft.

Made of wood, light metal or fibreglass, gliders derive their upward lift from vertical currents of air and hot air bubbles called thermals, which form above a hot piece of ground, like a field or farm building roof, when the temperature is right. As thermals rise, they increase in size, until it is possible for a glider to fly into a thermal and rise with it to a height of up to 6100 metres (20,000 feet).

WARPLANES SINCE THE SECOND WORLD WAR

Fighters

North American Sabre, USA
A single-seater fighter. Introduced by the US Air Force in 1949, it was their first swept-wing fighter and was used during the war in Korea. Powered by one turbo-jet, it had a maximum speed of 1102 kilometres (685 miles) per hour at sea level. A later version, the F-100 Super Sabre, is still in use.

Dassault Etendard IV, France
Brought into service by the French Air Force in 1956 as a low-level strike fighter. Powered by one turbo-jet, it was armed with two 30 mm. cannons. Later versions were adapted by the French Navy for use on aircraft carriers.

De Havilland Venom, Great Britain
An improved version of the earlier *Vampire*, the *Venom* was used by the Royal Air Force from 1949. From 1951 it was in service in Germany and the Middle East. Propelled by one turbo-jet, with a maximum speed of 1030 kilometres (640 miles) per hour, and a range of 1600 kilometres (1000 miles). The Royal Navy and the Fleet Air Arm used naval versions of it.

Fiat G91, Italy
Designed as a fighter for allied air forces in Europe, this aircraft first flew with the Italian Air Force in 1959. It is powered by one turbo-jet and can reach a maximum speed of 1075 kilometres (668 miles) per hour at sea level.

Gloster Javelin, Great Britain
The *Javelin*, designed as a two-seater fighter, first flew in 1951. It was powered by two turbo-jets and had a maximum speed of over 965 kilometres (600 miles) per hour. In the UK Javelins have now been replaced by more modern all-weather fighters.

McDonnell F-101 Voodoo, USA
Different models of this fighter-bomber provided one or two seats. The *Voodoo* first flew for Tactical Air Command in 1954, and later versions were used by Air Defense Command and the Royal Canadian Air Force. It was powered by two jet engines.

Yakovlev, USSR
A multi-fighter, powered by two turbo-jets, with a maximum speed of around 2090 kilometres (1300 miles) per hour. First appeared in an air show in 1961.

Saab-32 Lansen, Sweden
Designed as a two-seater, all-weather fighter, and first flown in 1952. It is powered by one turbo-jet and can reach a maximum speed of 1126 kilometres (700 miles) per hour at sea level. The Swedish Air Force is equipped with Lansens.

Mikoyan/Gurevich Mig-21, USSR
NATO code names are 'Fishbed' and 'Mongol'. A short-range delta-wing fighter first seen in Moscow in 1956. Is in wide use in the Czechoslovakian and other air forces. Has turbo-jet engines.

Convair Delta Dart, USA
A single-seater fighter of the 1950s, the *Delta Dart* was powered by one turbo-jet. This delta-wing plane was a development of the *F102 Delta Dagger*, and was in production from 1958.

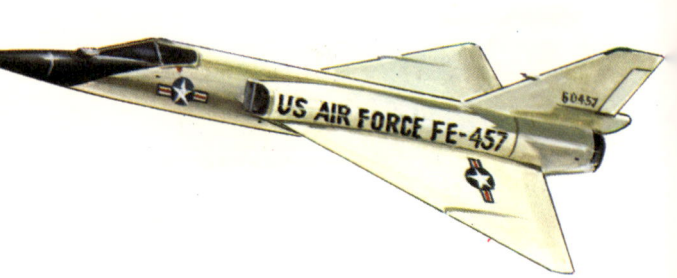

Lockheed Starfighter, USA
A small, Mach 2 single-seater interceptor-fighter, powered by one General Electric turbo-jet engine. This aircraft, which first appeared in 1954, is the basic military aeroplane of many of the world's air forces.

BAC Lightning, Great Britain
A single-seater fighter powered by two Rolls-Royce Avon jet engines, it has a speed of about 2400 kilometres (1500 miles) per hour. The *Lightning* is the front line fighter of the Royal Air Force.

Grumman Intruder, USA
A two-seater fighter and reconnaissance plane, powered by two jets and designed especially for use from aircraft carriers. The *Intruder* was first flown in 1960.

BAC/Aérospatiale Jaguar
Designed from 1965 by the British Aircraft Corporation and Breuget Aviation of France. A lightweight, high performance fighter, it has two versions—single seater and two-seater training version. Has two Rolls-Royce/Turbomeca Adour turbo-fan engines and bullet-proof windscreen.

Saab Viggen, Sweden
The *Viggen* is the latest Swedish military aircraft, and is a very powerful machine, being capable of speeds of about Mach 2. It is powered by one Swedish-built jet engine, and is being built in single-seater fighter versions and two-seat trainer versions for the Royal Swedish Air Force.

Bombers and Transport Planes

After the Second World War the idea of fleets of heavy bombers flying to their targets guarded by fighters was out of date, because bombers could now fly much faster and could also carry atomic bombs. Such bombs could do as much damage as all of the bombs of World War Two put together. Later on, bombers were to be replaced almost completely by rockets carrying atomic warheads, or bombs in their noses. But while wars *without* atomic bombs were still a possibility, there was still a need for jet bombers.

The high-speed transport aeroplane has an important role to play—it liaises with and gets supplies through to armies and air forces in distant countries, far outpacing slow, lumbering trucks and transport ships.

Here are some examples of bombers and transporters produced since World War Two:

Ilyushin IL-28, USSR
This four-seater light bomber was first seen in 1950 and is still in service. It is powered by two jets and has a maximum speed of about 930 kilometres (580 miles) per hour at 4570 metres (15,000 feet). Apart from the Soviet Air Force, it is in service with the air forces of many Eastern European countries and of China and Egypt. There are two fixed forward-firing automatic aircraft guns in the lower part of the nose and two machine guns in the tail turret.

Boeing Stratofreighter, USA
This design for a general transport and refuelling tanker aircraft was adapted for military use from the Boeing *Stratocruiser* transport. The two aircraft differ mainly in the arrangement and equipment of the large two-deck fuselage.

Avro Shackleton, Great Britain
Developed from the *Lincoln* bomber for reconnaissance and air-sea rescue service with Coastal Command, the *Shackleton* is equipped to carry torpedoes, mines and depth charges. It has been replaced by the H.S. *Nimrod*.

De Havilland Caribou, Canada
A light transport plane introduced into the Royal Canadian Air Force in 1958. Later, it was supplied to the United States Army. The *Caribou* is capable of short take-off and landing (STOL) which makes it very efficient in difficult terrain.

Handley Page Hastings, Great Britain
The *Hastings* was designed as a troop transport and general freighter, and went into service in 1948 with Transport Command. It had four propeller engines.

Tupolev Tu-16, USSR
Designed as a medium-range bomber, with twin jets and a maximum speed of around 950 kilometres (590 miles) per hour at 10,650 metres (35,000 feet) the *Tu-16* first appeared at a 1954 air show and has since been in service with the Soviet Air Force.

Blackburn Beverley, Great Britain
This aircraft was in use with the Royal Air Force from 1956. It accommodated 94 troops or 22 tons of freight. It could fly quite slowly, to allow troops or supplies to be dropped by parachute.

Douglas C-124 Globemaster, USA
The *Globemaster* was a very large transport plane, capable of carrying about 200 combat troops and a crew of eight.

Antonov, USSR
A medium-range transport powered by four turbo-props. Used chiefly for heavy freight and for dropping parachute troops. Designed for rear loading.

Boeing B-47 Stratojet, USA
One of the first swept-wing jet bombers in the world, the *B-47* was used by the US Air Force during and after the Korean war. Powered by six turbo-jets, it could carry up to 9100 kilogrammes (20,000 pounds) of bombs.

Canadair Yukon, Canada
This aircraft was designed as a long-range transport freighter for the Royal Canadian Air Force, and first flew in 1959. It is powered by four turbo-props and can carry 134 troops and a crew of five. Originally side-loading, it is now produced with a swing-tail to allow cargo to be loaded directly into the freight areas, this reduces loading time.

Dassault Mirage IV, France
This design was developed from the *Mirage III* fighter, for use by the French Air Force as a supersonic bomber. One nuclear weapon is carried beneath the fuselage.

Handley Page Victor, Great Britain
This medium-range bomber was designed for the Royal Air Force to carry up to 1600 kilogrammes (35,000 pounds) of bomb load. Powered by four turbo-jets, it has a maximum speed of 965 kilometres (600 miles) per hour. Later versions were converted to aerial fuel tankers.

Douglas Skyhawk, USA
A light, single-seater bomber designed for use with the US Navy on aircraft carriers. Powered by a single turbo-jet, it has a maximum speed of 1094 kilometres (680 miles) per hour at sea level.

General Dynamics Hustler, USA
A supersonic bomber powered by four turbo-jets. Operational aircraft were delivered to the US Air Force from spring 1960.

Hawker Siddeley Vulcan, Great Britain
The Royal Air Force first took deliveries of *Vulcan* bombers in 1956. There is provision for a crew of five. The aircraft was designed as a medium-range bomber, suitable for high or low level bombing, and has a maximum speed of 1000 kilometres (625 miles) per hour.

CIVIL AIRCRAFT

Airspeed indicator    *Horizontal situation indicator*    *Counter-pointer altimeter*

In 1919, when commercial air services started, there were few airlines and just as few aircraft to carry people. That first year, airlines carried a total of 3500 people, but by the start of World War Two they were accommodating about three million passengers every year in airliners which could cruise at 240 kilometres (150 miles) per hour and had seating for an average of eighteen people. Nowadays, over 300 major airlines exist which carry more than 325 million passengers on regular services every year. More than 4000 airliners are in use with the big airlines, and the modern jumbo jets carry nearly 500 passengers each!

A big airliner today is a complicated and expensive piece of machinery which takes many hours of careful maintenance to keep it flying smoothly. Some of the big aircraft are so heavy that it seems no engine could ever be powerful enough to lift them up into the sky. But the four massive jet engines with which they are usually equipped could easily supply the power requirements of a small town. From the safety point of view, it is interesting to know that a jumbo jet Boeing 747 could fly on the power of one engine if the the other three were to fail. And it could *climb* on the power of two engines. This model is in fact one of the safest airliners in the world.

Among the many instruments and aids a modern airliner carries, the flying instruments are the most important. These indicate that the aircraft is being flown correctly; they include the airspeed indicator, altimeter, turn and bank indicator, artificial horizon, compass and Machmeter. Then there are the engine instruments, which indicate fuel consumption, engine speed, engine temperatures and hydraulic pressures.

Although a pilot will know how to operate all

41

of the instruments mentioned he will *not* be able to fly from one point to another without a number of navigational aids. These include his compass, radio and radar. The pilot is in constant radio contact with the ground—helped by some advanced communications systems which operate on very high frequency. One of these is called VOR. Another, known as DME (Distance Measuring Equipment), is used by the pilot to calculate his distance and direction in relation to an airport. With such aids, he is able to fly across country, from airport to airport.

One system of vital importance in assisting the pilot to land in poor visibility is called Instrument Landing Systems (ILS). Transmitters on the ground are used to send signals to the aircraft, which the pilot can follow. He lines up his aircraft with the signals, and flies along a radio beam to a glide path. When he is on the glide path he can fly at a safe angle down to the airport runway. In the cockpit the attitude of the aircraft in relation to the signals is shown on a dial. When the pilot flies the aircraft correctly in response to the signals, the little aircraft on the dial lines up correctly with the markings.

At the airport, ground radar is used to help the pilot further, and as he comes into range his aircraft signal is picked up on the radar screen in the form of a little moving blip or form. With Precision Approach Radar (PAR), the pilot can be directed right over the airport.

A combination of ILS, radio altimeters and advanced automatic landing equipment can enable an aircraft to land today when it is impossible to see anything from the cockpit window. A British system called Autoland combines these aids for the pilot. Once on the ground, he can be directed further by a radar device called ASMI, or Airfield Surface Movement Indicator.

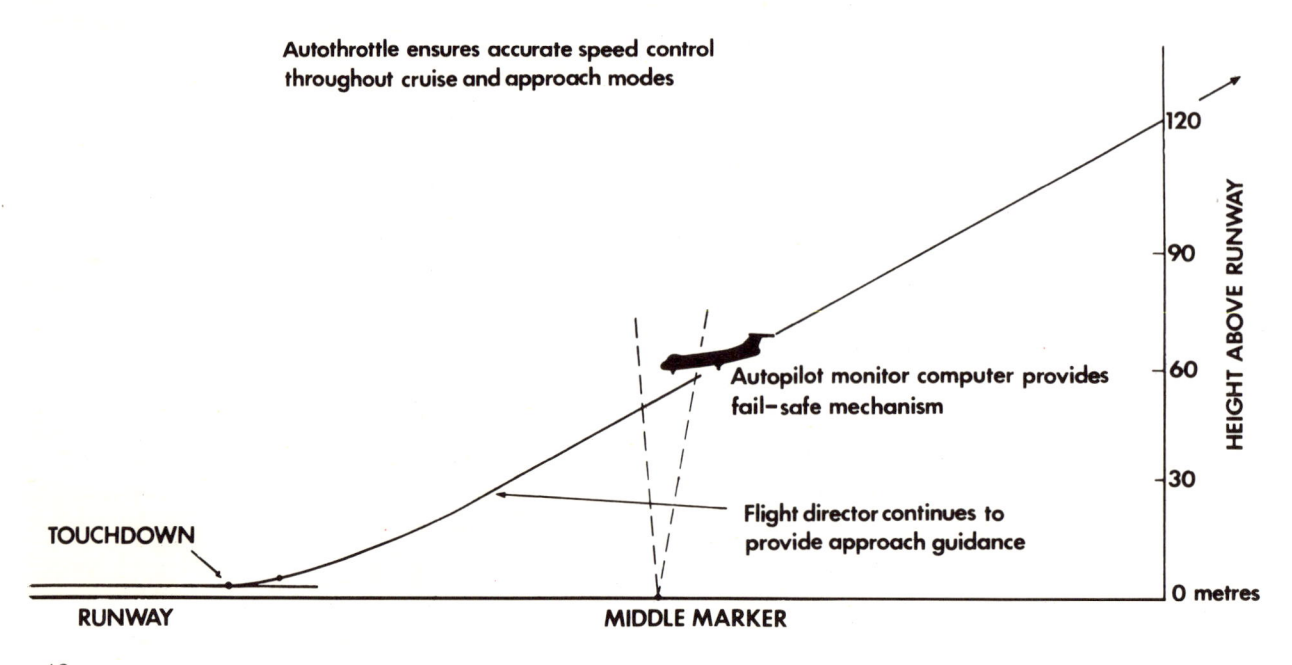

Autothrottle ensures accurate speed control throughout cruise and approach modes

Autopilot monitor computer provides fail-safe mechanism

Flight director continues to provide approach guidance

TOUCHDOWN
RUNWAY
MIDDLE MARKER
HEIGHT ABOVE RUNWAY
0 metres / 30 / 60 / 90 / 120

42

CATERING

Civil aviation today is a world-wide business employing many thousands of people. The jobs they do range from engineering, aircraft maintenance, engine repair and overhaul work, aircraft cleaning, ticket office work and the training of pilots, stewardesses and ground staff.

One important task involves the preparation of food and drink for passengers and crews. This highly specialized job is carried on in flight kitchens all over the world. Fresh supplies of ready cooked food are taken on board for each flight, and the air hostess and steward heat it in the galley ovens, so that passengers in flight are able to enjoy a hot meal.

Many big airlines have contracts with catering firms to supply the food, while others have their own, like Scandinavian Airlines System, which each year provides more than *five million* hot and cold meals for its passengers. SAS catering also supplies food and beverages for 40 other airlines, and has kitchens in several different countries.

Food can range from very ordinary bacon and eggs or steaks, to Scandinavian open sandwiches, Chinese and Oriental food, and hotly spiced curries. All kinds of tastes have to be catered for, and they are.

Above: Economy Class cabin of a British Airways 707. Below: In-flight meal service in the First Class cabin of a British Airways 707

Opposite: Flight landing path

AIRLINERS

Airliners of the world have developed considerably in size, speeds and range since World War Two. It is interesting to compare the old DC-3, which first flew in America in 1935 and needed to make several stops when flying across the United States, with the world's first jet airliner, the De Havilland Comet 1, which could carry 36 passengers; or again, with the 490-seat Boeing 747 of today, which can fly for almost 9650 kilometres (6000 miles) with a full load. In the past few years, aeroplanes have also become much more expensive to buy, although cheaper to operate. The old DC-3, for instance, cost £25,000 to buy, while the Boeing 747 costs a staggering £10,000,000!

Douglas DC-3, USA
Well over 10,000 *DC-3s* were built and many were used as short-haul military transports and later converted to passenger use by airlines, particularly for local and domestic routes. Cruising speed 255 kilometres (160 miles) per hour.

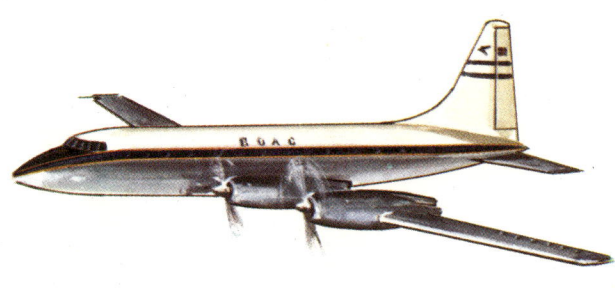

Bristol Britannia, Great Britain
Introduced into service in 1957, the *Britannia* was called the Whispering Giant because of the quietness of its engines. Powered by four turbo-prop engines giving a cruising speed of 563 kilometres (350 miles) per hour at 8530 metres (28,000 feet), it accommodates 95 passengers.

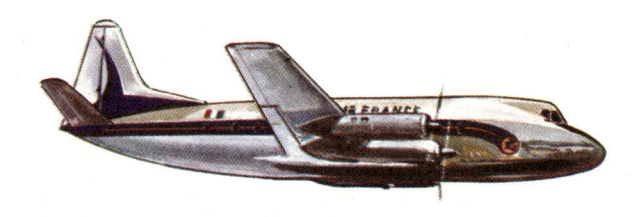

Vickers Viscount, Great Britain
First flown in 1948, the *Viscount* went into service with British European Airways in April 1953, as the first turbo-prop airliner in the world. There have been constant improvements in design, and many are still in use. Over 400 were sold.

Douglas DC-6, USA
A highly successful piston-engined airliner, powered by four 2500 hp piston engines, and still in service in many parts of the world. Cruising speed about 460 kilometres (285 miles) per hour at 2000 metres (6560 feet) and maximum seating capacity 73.

Boeing 707, USA
This was the first jet airliner built and flown in the United States, and was especially designed for operating across the North Atlantic Ocean. Equipped as an all-tourist class plane it provides seats for 189 passengers. Its maiden flight was on 15th July 1954, since when hundreds of orders have been delivered to airline operators all over the world. There are eight basic civil aviation models.

Fokker Friendship, Netherlands
The first prototype of this plane flew in 1955. The Dutch designed it as a medium-sized airliner to cover medium distances. It is powered by two turbo-props; the cruising speed is 440 kilometres (275 miles) per hour at 7000 metres (20,000 feet) and it can seat up to 56 passengers.

De Havilland Comet 1, Great Britain
Introduced as the world's first jet airliner in 1949, the *Comet 1* entered service with BOAC in May 1952. The bigger and better *Comet 4* went into passenger service on the North Atlantic in October 1958 with great success. It could carry up to 80 passengers for longer journeys, or a maximum of 102 on shorter trips.

Sud-Aviation Caravelle, France
The unusual design of the *Caravelle* was planned in 1951: two jet engines were placed in pods at the rear end of the fuselage. Chief advantages of this design were improved efficiency of the wings, reduction of noise and vibration in the cabin, and less risk of fire. The standard accommodation is for up to 64 first class passengers, and up to 80 tourist class.

Tupolev 104, USSR
Powered by two turbojets the *Tu-104* has a cruising speed of about 800 kilometres (500 miles) per hour and a range of 2650 kilometres (1650 miles). It seats 70 passengers. This was Russia's first turbo-jet airliner. It flew for the first time in 1955 and went into service with the Russian airline Aeroflot in September 1956.

Antonov 10, USSR
Powered by four turbo-prop engines, this is a civil development of a Russian freighter. One of the prototypes held seats for 84 passengers, divided into three cabins, with a playroom for children at the rear. The plane first flew in 1957 and is used mostly on internal routes in the Soviet Union.

Tupolev 114, USSR
One of the largest airliners ever flown, with accommodation for up to 220 passengers, on two decks. The galley is situated on a separate deck beneath the passenger lounges and food is sent up to the passengers by lift. The prototype of this plane first flew in 1958.

Handley Page Herald, Great Britain
The *Herald* was first powered by four engines, but the final version has two **R**olls-**R**oyce turbo-props. It has accommodation for up to 56 passengers.

Vickers Vanguard, Great Britain
First flew in January 1959. Powered by four turbo-prop engines with a cruising speed of 725 kilometres (450 miles) per hour. The *Vanguard* has a 'double-bubble' fuselage which means that it can carry a maximum of 139 tourist class passengers on the **upper deck, and 4630 kilogrammes (8000 pounds)** of freight in the two lower-deck cargo compartments. This plane was a follow-on to the successful *Viscount* design.

Douglas DC-8, USA
The first jet airliner produced by this company. *Series 10* was the first domestic version and went into service in 1959. The first five versions had an identical airframe. Intercontinental models differed from the domestic ones only in having a greater fuel capacity. Larger versions seating up to 260 were later built. A total of 550 *DC-8s* were sold.

BAC VC-10, Great Britain
Construction work on the first prototype began in 1959. The *VC-10* went into service with BOAC in April 1964. Powered by four jets housed in pods at the rear of the fuselage, the aircraft has accommodation for 152 passengers. The tailplane is mounted at the top of the fin.

Hawker Siddeley Trident, Great Britain
Design commenced in 1957 and the first *Trident* flew in 1962. The aircraft is powered by three jet engines—one each side and one above the rear part of the fuselage. The Trident was the first airliner to be designed and equipped for fully automatic landings. Initially it was ordered to meet the requirements for a short-haul 960 kmph (600 mph) airliner. It seats up to 139.

NAMC YS-11, Japan
A short-range aircraft powered by two turbo-props, the *YS-11* first flew in 1962. There is accommodation for up to 60 passengers, and the maximum cruising speed at 4570 metres (15,000 feet) is 480 kilometres (297 miles) per hour.

Convair 880, USA
There were two versions of this aircraft, the second being the *Convair 990*. It is used by a number of airlines, and is very fast, with a cruising speed of 985 kmph (615 mph). Its maximum cruising altitude is 13,000 metres (40,000 feet).

Dassault Fan Jet Falcon, France
This is a smaller, executive style aircraft, powered by twin turbofans and with accommodation for ten passengers and a crew of two. There is a small baggage compartment and wardrobe space. Prototype first flew in 1964. Cruising speed 750 kilometres (470 miles) per hour. Used by Air France to train their jet pilots, a modified version is used by the French air force to train their fighter pilots.

Canadair 400, Canada
Powered by four turbo-prop engines, this aircraft was a Canadian-designed version of the *Britannia* airliner. Several are in service, seating about 180 passengers.

Lockheed TriStar, USA
In service in the USA and Europe, the *TriStar* has three Rolls-Royce RB211 engines. Prototype first flew in 1970. It can seat up to 400 passengers in the cabin and there are large cargo bays under the passenger deck. Maximum cruising speed at 10,000 metres (30,000 feet) is 960 kilometres (600 miles) per hour.

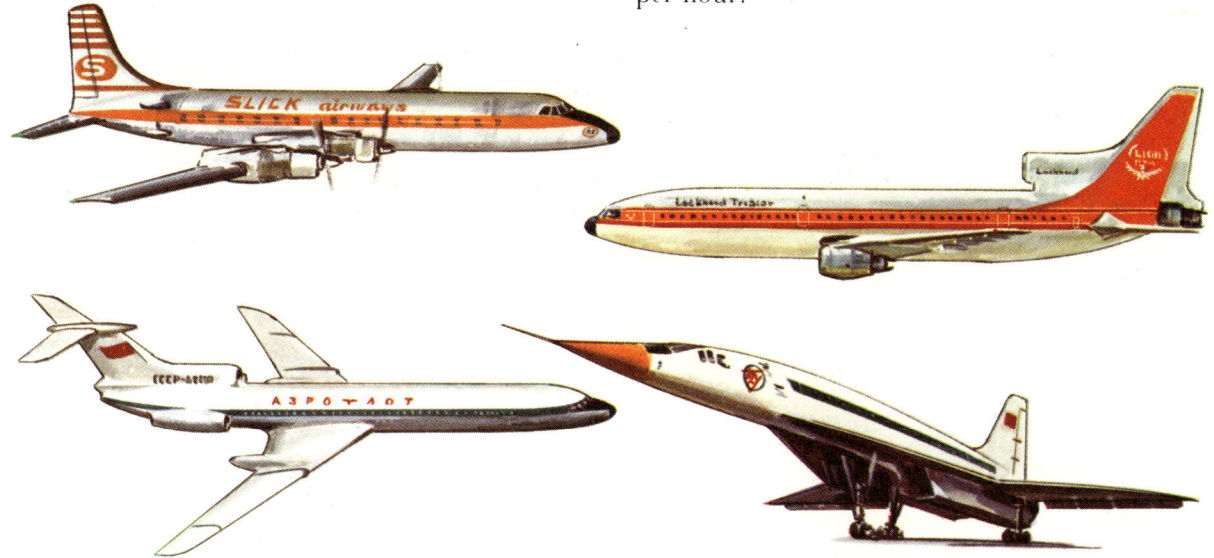

Tupolev 154, USSR
This three-engined medium/long-range jet was first announced in the spring of 1966. It is similar to the *Trident* and the Boeing 727 and is a production aircraft for Aeroflot. There are several basic passenger versions with maximum seating for 164. There is also an all-cargo version. Maximum cruising speed at 10,000 metres (30,000 feet) is 970 kilometres (605 miles) per hour. A lengthened version, the *Tu-154M*, accommodating 230–240 passengers is under development.

Tupolev 144, USSR
This supersonic passenger aircraft resembles the Anglo-French *Concorde* in outward appearance. Its nose is movable to give better visibility on landing. First displayed at the Paris Air Show in 1967. Fitted out to provide a 100-seat arrangement.

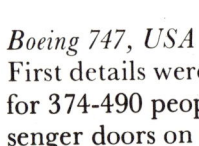

Boeing 747, USA
First details were released in 1966. With capacity for 374-490 people, this 'Jumbo' jet has five passenger doors on each side. Powered by four Pratt & Whitney JT9D engines. There is an all-cargo version which can transport up to 200,000 pounds of containerized cargo.

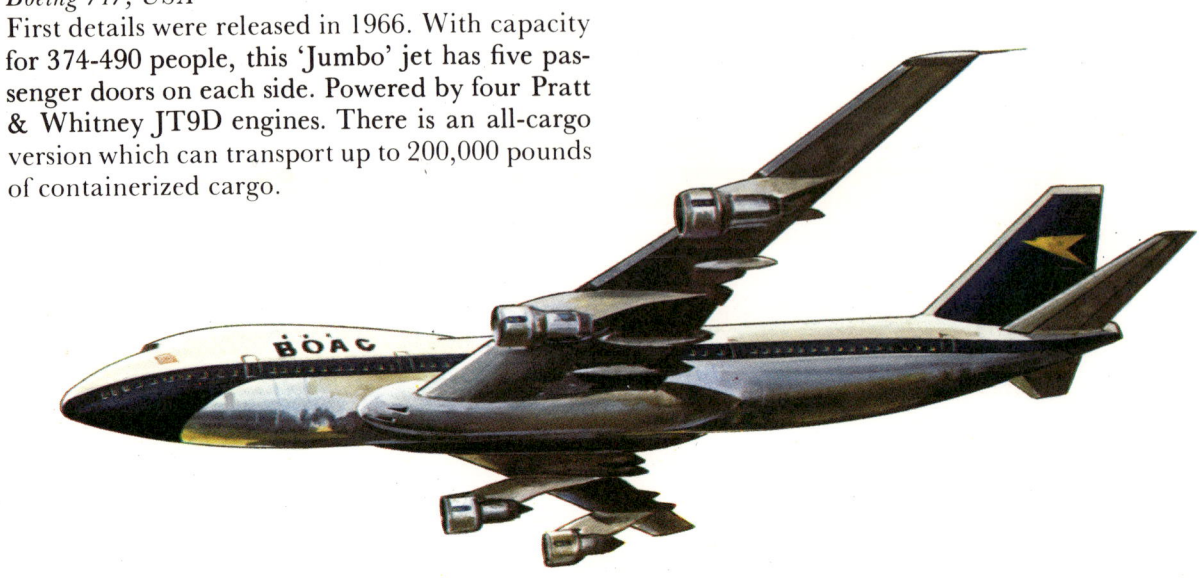

McDonnell Douglas DC-10, USA
First manufactured in 1969 and assembled in California. Powered by three General Electric CF6-6D turbofan engines. Intended for service on world routes of between 3200 and 9650 kilometres (2000–6000 miles). There is also a convertible cargo version, the Model 30F. High class catering and luxury seating for 255–345 passengers.

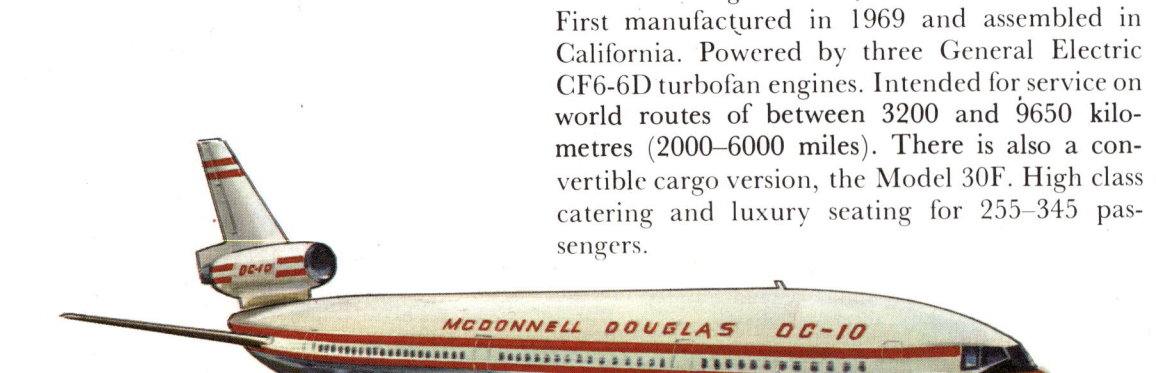

SUPERSONIC PASSENGER FLIGHT

Concorde

We have repeatedly seen how man has always wanted to fly, and to fly *fast*. One speed record has been followed by another, and so on . . . until speed as such has almost lost its meaning. Man has achieved speed enough to free him from the Earth's gravitational pull, and take him out into space.

We on Earth live beneath the invisible layer of the atmosphere, and are concerned with its density. When flying through the atmosphere, powerful engines are required to speed heavy airliners across the world. The jet engine made the high-speed airliner possible; the next step was to build an airliner which could fly as fast as a military fighter or at very high Mach numbers, that is—at supersonic speeds. So a design for a supersonic airliner was drawn up, in Great Britain, but the cost was so high that her government decided to share the project with France—hence the birth of the Anglo-French Concorde—the world's first supersonic airliner.

The British Aircraft Corporation in Britain and Sud-Aviation in France (now called Aérospatiale), signed an agreement in November 1962 to build and sell Concordes to the world's airlines. After more than ten years of design, construction work and test flying, the Concorde is nearly ready to enter commercial service with the first two airlines to order it—British Airways and Air France.

What are the advantages of supersonic travel? Well, people can reach distant lands very quickly, and as far as airlines are concerned, this means more passengers can be carried in a given time—which means that airlines can make more money. Let us look at the journey round the world. In 1949, it took about 132 hours to fly right around the world, a distance of about 40,000 kilometres (25,000 miles). When Pan American World Airways introduced jet airliners on its round-the-world service in 1959, the journey time was reduced to 80 hours. Today, the journey can be flown in 65 hours. To the traveller, this means a quicker arrival in a foreign country and more time to spend there, on either business or pleasure. That is why airlines like fast aircraft, and why passengers like them too. And that is why supersonic airliners will be successful when they start operating.

The Concorde design was followed by a Russian version, the Tupolev Tu-144, which had in fact made its maiden flight before Concorde, on 31 December 1968. (Concorde first flew in February 1969.) In America, too, the Boeing Company and Lockheed Aircraft Corporation had designed 'SSTs', but the building of the Boeing aircraft was deferred for economic reasons. It would have been much bigger than Concorde, and would have flown faster.

Concorde's speed will be Mach 2·2, around 2400 kilometres (1500 miles) per hour at its cruising height of approximately 16,750 metres (55,000 feet). A special protective visor will slide up over the cockpit windows to protect the glass and also to produce a much smoother aerodynamic shape to the airflow as the aircraft rushes through the sky.

On landing, Concorde's nose will lower, or droop, to give the pilot a clear view of the ground. The reason for this is the delta shape of Concorde's wing, which means that it must approach to land at a steep angle, blocking the pilot's view unless he lowers the nose.

Concorde will carry 120 passengers in its first version, and will fly non-stop, in about two and a half hours, across the North Atlantic. At present, the journey on that route takes seven hours. Concorde is powered by four Olympus turbo-jet engines, and will weigh about 145 tons. It should enter airline service in 1975.

Concorde controls

ROCKET-POWERED CRAFT

Martin X-24A

Northrop HL.10 built for NASA

North American Aviation Inc. X-15

Ever since the Chinese invented gunpowder the rocket has seemed an attractive form of propellant for a number of reasons. It is the fastest type of propulsion that man can use for transporting a load—be it a bomb or himself—from one place to another. Gunpowder is no longer used, of course, but a number of different gases or chemicals ranging from liquid oxygen to ammonia, alcohol and boron. When combinations of these fuels are mixed, the result is a tremendously powerful explosive propellant which is capable of driving an enormously heavy rocket at very great speed.

The most obvious use of rockets is in war. The Russians were among the first to use rocket weapons, in World War Two. One of the first rocket powered aircraft was the American Bell X-1, which exceeded sonic speed on 14 October 1947. The Bell X-1 was carried into the air by another aircraft, a four-engined Boeing Superfortress, and at 9140 metres (30,000 feet) its rocket motor was ignited and it was released from the mother craft. Colonel Charles Yeager was the principal pilot of this aircraft, and by 1953 the X-1 was reaching fantastic speeds of up to 2655 kilometres (1650 miles) per hour. It was joined by another rocket powered aircraft of a similar type, called the Douglas Skyrocket. The Skyrocket was similarly very fast, and once attained the incredible height of 32 kilometres (20 miles). It differed from the Bell as it could take off from the ground under its own power.

Further research continued in the USA with manned rocket powered craft, and the most remarkable results were achieved with a machine called the North American X-15. This, again, had to be carried into the air by a mother ship, but this enabled it to save fuel for its high-speed dashes. The X-15 had smaller wings than a World War Two Spitfire, but from the time it first flew in 1959, it started to notch up incredible speeds and heights. By 1965, when designers were seriously planning to go to the moon with wingless space craft, the X-15 had flown at over six times the speed of sound, or 6600 kilometres (4100 miles) per hour, and to the fantastic height of 114 kilometres (71 miles). One of the pilots of the X-15 was Neil Armstrong, the first man to land on the moon.

For military purposes, rockets are used today as prime aerial weapons. They can carry explosive warheads weighing many tons over thousands of kilometres, and if necessary can carry atomic bombs.

A rocket fired from an underground pit in one country can be guided halfway across the world to crash on a city and completely destroy it, without the launcher of the rocket ever showing himself to the enemy. There is really no defence against this kind of warfare, although missiles designed to blow up another in mid-air have been designed and built.

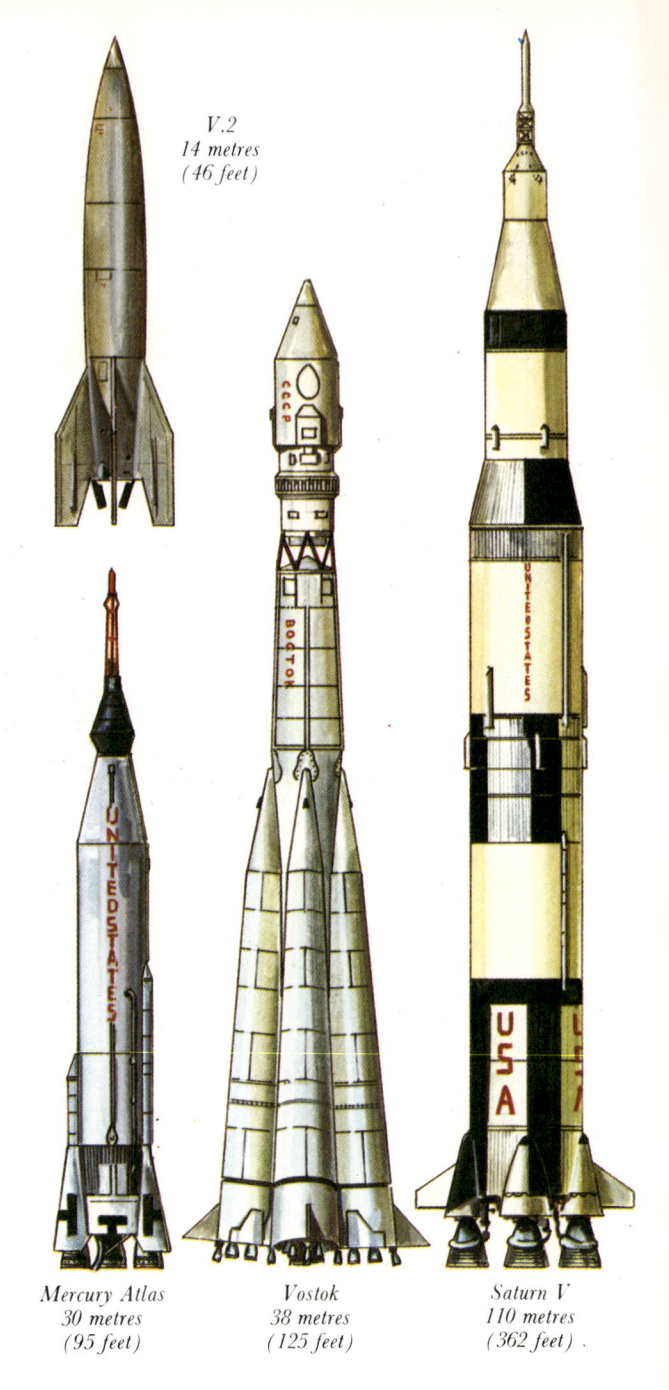

V.2
14 metres
(46 feet)

Mercury Atlas
30 metres
(95 feet)

Vostok
38 metres
(125 feet)

Saturn V
110 metres
(362 feet)

THE SPACE AGE

What we now call the Space Age began on 4 October 1957 when an astonished world was told that a man-made satellite was orbiting the Earth. For the first time in history man had sent out into the atmosphere a rocket, which had released a small sphere about the same size as a football, and which was now flying, like the Earth, suspended in space.

This first satellite was launched by the Russians, who after the war had concentrated on building powerful rockets, with both military and space purposes in mind. The military aspect was of particular importance, since the Germans had previously recognized the rocket as a means of destroying cities without using manned aircraft. The explosive-carrying rocket is much more destructive than an aircraft bomber.

The Russians now embarked on a programme of space exploration, the initial objective of which was to fly to the moon. For some years the Americans too had been experimenting—with captured German wartime rockets—but their programme of space research was moving slowly. Only when Sputnik, the first satellite, started orbiting did America accelerate its space research programme. President John F. Kennedy announced that America's new objective would be to put a man on to the moon 'before the end of the decade', which meant by 1970.

Almost at once, the National Aeronautics and Space Administration was formed, and many thousands of engineers, scientists and technicians were signed up for jobs and millions of dollars were allocated to the American space programme.

One objective was to explore space with unmanned vehicles, and this was done by a number of satellites similar to Sputnik and increasingly larger. The Russians and Americans were at this time working more or less on parallel lines. The next step was to put a man into space, and this the Russians achieved in 1961 by launching Major Yuri Gagarin in a satellite to orbit the Earth. The following year, in Project Mercury, Major John Glenn of the United States Air Force made three orbits of the Earth in the first American manned satellite. The Gemini programme followed, in which two American astronauts went into space together. The two-man Gemini spacecraft astonished the world with films of one of the astronauts leaving the craft and walking in space —160 kilometres (100 miles) above the Earth. There is no atmosphere in space and no gravity, and consequently a body just floats about as if in water. Because there is no air, the astronauts have to wear special suits, with breathing equipment inside.

The American Apollo programme was next. Three men were fired into space in a capsule on the top of a rocket, and when the capsule had separated from the main rocket and flown into space on its own, the men orbited the moon. The Russians were working along the same lines with their Soyuz spacecraft. By now, it seemed that Russia and the United States were competing in a space race, to see who could reach the moon first.

On 20 July 1969—eighteen months before President Kennedy's deadline—two American astronauts, Neil Armstrong and Edwin Aldrin, landed on the moon in their LEM, or Lunar Excursion Module, and Neil Armstrong became the first man ever to set foot on another planet. The Russians have never landed a man on the moon, although they have made a number of gallant attempts to do so. In future, it is likely that the United States and Russia will join scientific and economic forces to explore the planets and outer space together.

The rocket which took the first American team of Armstrong, Aldrin and Collins to the moon was a Saturn V rocket, and like the others was based on a military rocket design. The Saturn V had several stages, containing mostly fuel: when these tanks or stages burned out, they fell away, leaving the Apollo spacecraft finally free to fly to the moon on its own. Inside were the three men with their mooncraft, which took them right down to the moon's surface. After they had returned from the moon to the main craft they left their landing craft behind.

Since then, there have been several more flights to the moon. The last was Apollo 17, which is said to be the final flight to the moon in this century. But the Saturn V rocket, the most powerful flying machine ever built, and which weighs 3000 tons on take-off from the Earth, will continue to be used for carrying other spacecraft into orbit.

One such craft is Skylab, an experimental space laboratory launched on 16 May 1973. The initial difficulties encountered with Skylab were overcome and it carried several men in orbit round the Earth. It is not intended to go to the moon and the astronauts perform various scientific tasks and stay for periods of time, living, sleeping and working. Long distance space travel of the future will probably take the form of flying from one spacecraft to another anchored in space. Skylab is the first research space stepping stone of this kind.

Another method of space travel is called the space shuttle. Winged craft, like aeroplanes, attached to the launching rocket, will be used to make space journeys after the launching rocket has done its job. The shuttle craft will be able to return through the atmosphere and fly right back down to Earth.

57

DIARY OF IMPORTANT DATES

15 October 1783	First ascent by man—in a balloon
January 1785	First crossing of the English Channel by balloon
1876	Invention of the first four stroke internal combustion engine by Otto in Germany
1891	Otto Lilienthal in Germany becomes the first man to glide on wings
1893	Lawrence Hargrave invents the box-kite in Australia
1898	Alberto Santos-Dumont makes the first of his 14 airships, and flies in France
1900	Two American brothers, Orville and Wilbur Wright make their first glider flights
17 December 1903	The first powered, controlled and sustained man-carrying, heavier-than-air flight in the USA by the Wright brothers
23 October 1906	The first aeroplane flight in Europe by Santos-Dumont
June 1908	A. V. Roe is the first Englishman to fly in England
25 July 1909	First crossing of the English Channel by aeroplane by Louis Blériot
1 April 1918	Founding of the British Royal Air Force
25 August 1919	First commercial air service begun between London and Paris
14–15 June 1919	First crossing of the Atlantic by aeroplane
10 December 1919	First flight from England to Australia completed
1924	Formation of Imperial Airways, later BOAC, now British Airways
May 1927	First solo flight of the Atlantic by Charles Lindbergh
1933	First solo round-the-world flight by Wiley Post
1939	First trans-Atlantic flying-boat service inaugurated
1939	Flight of the world's first jet aircraft, the Heinkel 178
May 1941	First flight of British jet aircraft, Gloster E28/39
2 May 1952	World's first jet airliner service started by BOAC
1959	Round-the-world jet airliner services begun
February 1969	First flight of the Concorde supersonic airliner
20 July 1969	First landing of man on the moon, Neil Armstrong and Edwin Aldrin

GLOSSARY

ATC *Air traffic control*

Atmosphere *The invisible skin which covers the Earth and which encloses the air we breathe*

Automatic Landing *In which equipment controls and directs the aircraft without manual effort by the pilot*

BEA *British European Airways*

Biplane *An aeroplane with two wings, one above the other*

BOAC *British Overseas Aircraft Corporation*

Capsule *The crew's quarters on board a space vehicle*

Hypersonic *Flight at many times the speed of sound, sometimes called ultra-sonic*

ILS *Instrument landing system*

LEM *Lunar excursion module*

Let-down *The first step to landing*

Lift-off *The take-off of a rocket following ignition*

Long-range *Aircraft or missile designed to fly specifically over long distances, and carrying enough fuel to do so without landing*

LRV *Lunar roving vehicle*

Monoplane *A single-winged aeroplane, or one with a wing on either side of the fuselage*

Multi-engined *Having three or more engines*

Orbit *A body in space following a course around the Earth or some other planet*

Powered Controls *Flying controls which have power assistance to help the pilot*

Ramjet *Jet engine driven by air rammed through it*

Shock-wave *Wave created by the very fast thrusting of an aircraft or missile through the air*

Short-range *Aircraft designed to fly over short distances*

SST *Supersonic transport*

STOL *Short take-off and landing*

Stratosphere *Region of high altitude, where the air is thin and where artificial aid to breathing is required because of oxygen deficiency*

Subsonic *Flight below the speed of sound*

Supersonic *Flight faster than the speed of sound—usually expressed as a Mach number—ie Mach 1·00*

Take-off *The start of a flight*

Transonic *Flight at the speed of sound*

Triplane *An aeroplane with three wings, one above the other*

Turbo-jet *Jet engine*

Turbo-prop *Jet engine driving a propeller*

Twin-engined *Two-engined aircraft*

VASI *Visual approach slope indicator*

VHF *Very high frequency radio*

VOR *VHF omni-directional radio*

VTOL *Vertical take-off and landing*

INDEX

A
A-300B 'Airbus' 8
Ader, Clément 14
Aeroflot 49
Aérospatiale. *See* Sud-Aviation
Air ambulance 29
Air France 51
Airliners 44–50
Airlines 18–19
Airspeed indicator 41
Alcock, John 19
Aldrin, Edwin 56
Altimeter 41
Antonov 39; '10', 46
Apollo programme 56
Arlandes, Marquis d' 11
Armstrong, Neil 54, 56
ASMI (Airfield Surface Movement Indicator) 42
Astronauts 56
Autoland 42
Avro Lancaster 22; 'Shackleton', 37

B
Beagle 29
Bell X-1 53–4
Biplanes 12
Blackburn Beverley 38
Bladud, king of Britain 10
Blanchard, J. P. 12
Blériot, Louis 14, 15, 18
Boeing 707 43, 45; 747 ('Jumbo Jet'), 41, 44, 50; 'Superfortress', 53
Bombers 36–40
Borton, Brigadier-General 19
Bristol 29; 'Britannia', 44
British Aircraft Corporation 51
British Airways 51
Brown, Arthur Whitten 19–20

C
Canadair 400 49
Caproni-Campini 23
Caravelle II 8, 46
Car-ferry 29
Caribou 37
Cavallo, Tiberius 11
Cavendish, Henry 11
Cayley, George 12
Chanute, Octave 13
Charles, J. A. C. 11
Cobham, Alan 19, 21
Concorde 8, 49, 51, 52
Convair Delta Dart 34; '880', 48
Coxwell, Henry 11
Crop-spraying 29
Curtiss, Glen 16
Curtiss NC-4 19

D
Daedalus 10
Dassault Etendard IV 31; Fan Jet Falcon, 48
Da Vinci, Leonardo 10, 11, 12, 28
De Conneau, J. 16
De Havilland B.E.2 16; Comet 1, 45; Comet 4, 45; Venom, 31
Demoiselle monoplane 14
Deperdussin monocoque 16; Racer, 8
DME 42
Dornier DO31E 8
Douglas C-124 Globemaster 38; DC-3, 44; DC-6, 45; DC-8, 47; DC-10, 50; Skyrocket, 54
Drachen balloon 12

E
Earhart, Amelia 21
Ellehammer, J. C. H. 15
Eole 14

F
F-101 Voodoo 32
Fiat G91 32
FIDO 23
Fighters 31–5
Flyer, The 13, 15
Flying Doctor Service 29
Flying Fortress 22
Fokker Friendship 45

G
Gagarin, Yuri 55
Gas turbine engine 23–5
Gemini programme 56
Gifford, Henry 11
Glenn, John 56
Gliders 12–13, 30
Gloster Javelin 32
Graf Zeppelin 20
Grahame-White, Claude 16
Grumman AGCAT 29; Intruder, 35

H
Halley, Lieutenant 19
Hamel, Gustav 16
Handley Page Hastings 37; Herald, 47
Hargrave, Lawrence 13
Hawker Siddeley Harrier 9
Hearst, William Randolph 16
Helicopters 10, 28–9
Hindenburg 20
Hinkler, H. J. 21
Horizontal situation indicator 41
Horsa glider 30
Hustler 40

I
Icarus 10
ILS (Instrument Landing Systems) 42
Ilyushin IL-28 36
Internal combustion engine 23

J
Jaguar 8, 35
Jeffries, Dr J. 12

Jet engine 23–5
Johnson, Amy 21
Jumbo Jet 41, 50
Junkers JU52/3M 8; JU88, 22

K
Kennedy, John F. 55

L
LEM (Lunar Excursion Module) 56
Leonardo. *See* Da Vinci
Lightning 34
Lilienthal, Otto 12
Lincoln 37
Lindbergh, Charles 21
Lockheed Aircraft Corporation 52

M
Mach, Ernst 27
Machmeter 27, 41
Maclaren, Major 19
Martin X-24A 53
Mercury Atlas 54
Mercury project 56
Messerschmitt 22
Mikoyan/Gurevich Mig-21 33
Mirage IV 40
Mitsubishi 22
Montgolfier, Joseph and Etienne 11
Moon, the 9

N
NAMC YS-11 48
NASA 55
Nimrod 37
North American Aviation X-15 53, 54
Northrop HL.10 53

O
Olympia 463 30
Ornithopter 10

P
Pan American 51
PAR (Precision Approach Radar) 42

Paulhan, Louis 15, 16
Piaggio 22
Pilâtre de Rozier J. F. 11
Pilcher, Percy 12
Pressurization 27
Prier, Pierre 16

R
R-34 airship 20
Radar 26
Read, Lt.-Commander 19
Rockets 23, 24, 25, 53
Rodgers, Galbraith 16
Roe, A. V. 15

S
Saab-32 Lansen 33; Viggen, 8, 35
Sabre 31
Santos-Dumont, Alberto 8, 14, 15
SAS 43
Saturn V 54, 56
Shun, Chinese emperor 10
Sikorsky, Igor 28
Sikorsky VS-300 16
Skeeter 6 28
Skyhawk 40
Skylab 56
Slingsby Skylark 30
Smith, Charles Kingsford 21
Smith, Keith 21
Smith, Captain Ross 19, 21
Sonic boom 27
Sopwith, Thomas 16
Sound barrier 27
Southern Cross 21
Soyuz 56
Space shuttle 56
Space travel 55–6
Spirit of St Louis 21
Spitfire 22
Sputnik 55
Starfighter 34
Stratofreighter 36
Stratojet 39
Sud-Aviation 51
Supersonic flight 51

T
Transport planes 36–40
Trident 48
TriStar 49
Tupolev Tu-16 38; Tu-104, 46; Tu-114, 46; Tu-144, 49, 52; Tu-154, 49

U
Ulm, Charles 21

V
V.2 54
Vampire 31
VC-10 47
Vickers Viscount 44; Vanguard, 47
Victor 40
Voisin brothers 15
Voisin biplane 14
Von Ohain, Hans 23
VOR 42
Vostok 54
VTOL 9, 29
Vulcan 40

W
Warplanes 31–40
Watson-Watt, Sir Robert 26
Whirlwind 28
Whispering Giant 44
Whittle, Frank 23, 25
Wright, Orville and Wilbur 13, 14–15, 16, 17, 23, 30

Y
Yakovlev 33
Yeager, Colonel Charles 53
Yukon 39

Z
Zeppelin, Count Ferdinand 20
Zeppelins 13, 17, 20